FROM SUSSEX YEOMEN
TO
GREENWICH WATERMEN

A W GEARING

To Robert: Fran & Family,
From one Gearing to another.

Albert

Nov. 2001

Country Books

Published by:
Country Books, Courtyard Cottage, Little Longstone, Derbyshire DE45 1NN

ISBN 1 898941 55 6

Design, typesetting & production:
Dick Richardson, Country Books, Little Longstone, Derbyshire DE45 1NN

THIS BOOK IS DEDICATED

TO THE MEMORY OF OUR BELOVED PARENTS

JACK AND MAY

ACKNOWLEDGEMENTS

East Sussex Record Office.

Public Record Office. Publishers of 'Sussex Coroners' Inquests', by R. Hunnisett.

Don. Burgess, who transcribed 'John Burgess's Journal'.

The Company of Waterman and Lightermen and Bob Crouch, Her Majesty's Bargemaster, for providing me with photographs and details of the Company.

Greenwich History Library for giving me access to the Greenwich Workhouse records, during the 1820's.

Eric de Mare, author of 'London's Riverside'.

Max Arthur, author of 'The True Glory'.

Neil Rhind, author of 'Blackheath and Environs'.

D. R. Morris, ex. master and author of 'The Royal Hospital School, Holbrook'.

Capt. Christopher Fagan, Chairman of The Gallipoli Association, for the moving address he gave at my fathers funeral.

My very good friend in war and peace, Peter Carrick, the author of several books, for the help and encouragement he gave me.

My cousin John Masterman the son of Sir Christopher, for the information he gave me about India. The local author, Mark Dudeney, for the advice he gave me, and David Twigge-Molecey, whose suggestion it was to write this book.

CONTENTS

INTRODUCTION   7

CHAPTER 1 – SUSSEX 1500 – 1795   9

CHAPTER 2 – GREENWICH 1795 – 1821   28

CHAPTER 3 – GREENWICH 1821 – 1844   43

CHAPTER 4 – GREENWICH 1844 – 1884   54

CHAPTER 5 – GREENWICH 1884 – 1914   69

CHAPTER 6 – THE GREAT WAR 1914 – 1922   77

CHAPTER 7 – CHILDHOOD MEMORIES 1922 – 1939   90

CHAPTER 8 – THE WAR YEARS 1939 – 1947   120

CHAPTER 9 – 1947 – 1985   134

CHAPTER 10 – FOLKESTONE 1985 – 1997   157

FAMILY TREE   176

INTRODUCTION

I do not claim to be a historian, but have always had a great interest in English history. Therefore, I have been very fortunate, to have been able to trace my family through the male line back to the Middle ages. In the course of research, I was able to find out quite a lot about them in each generation starting from 1500. I hope it will give the reader a glimpse of what life was like for an ordinary English person during each century.

In the 16th.century, my family led fairly comfortable lives as Yeomen in Sussex. As such, they were sometimes called upon to do jury service at the Coroner's Inquests, this gave me an opportunity to describe how brutal, short and hard, life could be at that time.

During the beginning of the 17th.century, when people were being persecuted for joining the various religious denominations, which were springing up, my family became Baptists. To avoid being imprisoned or even worse they had to meet secretly in each other's barns. They continued to do this until the end of the century, when an 'Act of Toleration', was passed.

During the 18th.century, they were smallholders and craftsmen. Now they were able to worship freely at a Baptists' Meeting House, which had been built in the village of Ditchling in Sussex, where they were living. The lay preacher at the Chapel was a friend of the family, and he kept a diary in the

1780's, in which he mentioned the Gearing's quite a lot. This journal describes what every day life was like in rural Britain at that time.

At the beginning of the 19th century my great-great-great grandfather had moved to Greenwich. His son joined Nelson's Navy when he was twelve and came out at the age of sixteen. His father then apprenticed him as a Waterman and Lighterman on the Thames. In 1820, this son married, but could not find work, and their first son, was born in Greenwich Workhouse. I have had access to the Workhouse reports of what life was like there, which I have described. Fortunately they did not have to stay there very long. From then on, every son was apprenticed to the River.

Some of them then sought their fortune elsewhere, one settled in India, another in Australia, going there at the time of the 1850's gold rush, My grandfather also spent four years in Australia; after travelling all over China, Japan and visiting several other countries, including America. He was born in the 1850's, and died at ninety, so I remember him well, and he could tell me a lot about his father and grandfather, who was born in 1798. My father lived to 102 and died in 1997. Both of them used to tell me what Greenwich and life on the river was like in their time, which included the Great War. And I remember what it was like living in London during the Blitz and later in the Army in the 1939-1945 War.

CHAPTER ONE

SUSSEX 1500 – 1795

My family's association with Greenwich, began in 1795, when Henry Gearing arrived from Sussex. The Gearing's had lived in Sussex for generations, the name is first found in the 'The Subsidy Rolls' of Sussex of 1296, as Sewal Geryng, but I have always been given to understand, the name is of Saxon origin, so they probably arrived here after the Romans left in about 600AD Sussex or "South Saxony', was one of their strongholds.

During the Middle Ages, they were Yeomen, farming the land surrounding the little fishing village of Brighton, which was then called Brightelmeston.

In the 15th and 16th centuries, they were living somewhere between Withdean and Patcham, about five miles north of Brighton, at the foot of the South Downs.

At the beginning of the 16th century, when Henry VIII was a boy, Richard Geeringe was born, and his father was a Yeoman. In 1532, young Richard married a young lady named Margaret, they had a son also named Richard, who was born in 1533. When he grew up, he followed in his father's footsteps, and eventually took over on the death of his father in 1561. Also in that year he married Elizabeth, their first born son was also called Richard, born in 1562, followed by three more children.

Their father increased the fortunes of the family. His name

often appears in the 'Abstract of Sussex Deeds', to do with property transactions. In 1570, he was assigned the lease of the "Prebend of Exceat', an ecclesiastical document, which entitled him to the lands, tithes, oblations etc. belonging to the village of Exceat in the Parish of West Dean, for eighty years, at a rent of £5.8.6d. The prebend had been granted to the vicars of Exceat, by the Bishop of Chichester, in the Middle Ages. Unfortunately, most of the occupants of the village had died during the "Black Death' of 1348, after which the village was deserted, and fell into ruin, until it disappeared and no longer exists, so the income would have come from the land, such as grazing rights etc.

During the 1570's, 80's and 90's the Geeringe family often served as Jurors at the "Sussex Coroners' Inquests'. In 1570 Richard had to attend with his three sons and others, at the inquest of John Peache, aged 18, who feloniously hanged himself in the barn of his master, with a "trayce worth 2d died immediately and had no goods or chattels.

In 1578 they appeared at the inquest of John Johnson, a carpenter, who was removing a piece of wood called a "Wale Plate'. When it fell from the house and broke his left leg, whereby he died immediately.

In 1592 they attended another inquest on George Harts, a boy, was in a meadow near a pit, looking at the water of the pit, he stabbed at a 'post' in the water with a "hedgingge byll' and by misadventure, fell into the water and was drowned. No one else was guilty of his death. He had no goods or chattels.

Some of the other inquests were quite tragic, in 1562, John the son of William Purdew, aged over 6, was at William Spookes, his step-father, who took hold of him, bound his hands and feet, and hung him up by the shins, struck him, giving him many wounds, so that blood fell from his body to the ground. As he lay there, Spookes struck, punched and trampled on him, crushing his body. John lay languishing in his bed until the next day, and then died at 10 am. Spookes then dug a hole in his barn, and buried John's body in it with his face downwards. Spookes was outlawed at Lewes and later pardoned.

In Feb. 1553. Richard Barnerde of Hellingly, copulated with his daughter Joan, who conceived and gave birth to a girl, without the company of women. Afterwards, Richard took the infant in his hands, and hid her under a tub, and placed a mallet. on her chest and murdered her. The next day, reflecting on his horrible crime, he went to a well and feloniously drowned himself. He had goods and chattels worth £12.13.8d.

In Nov. 1555, Robert Kent and Elizabeth his wife, sent their daughter Agnes, aged 6, to guard and control a flock of sheep belonging to George Gorringe, Gent. in his pasture. She was there all night, and died of the cold, she took through her parents negligence in that they took no care of her. This was classified as a natural death.

Petworth, 1569. On 29th June, a quarrel arose between Robert Mose of Tillington, 'Taylor', and Thomas Sadler late of Petworth, 'shoemaker', at Petworth over 2d. which Mose demanded from Sadler, and Mose thereupon took Sadlers hat and carried it off. Later that day, when Mose was going towards his house at Tillington with Sadler pursuing him, by running more quickly, Sadler caught him in Petworth, and struck him in the head with a knife from which Mose fell to the ground. Getting up again, he leapt upon Sadler and feloniously killed him with Sadler's dagger. Which during the struggle, he withdrew from its sheath and held in his right hand, giving him a deep wound in his left ribs so that it cut his intestines, of which Sadler languished until July 5th when he died. Mose had no goods or chattels. He pleaded not guilty, but was convicted. He then successfully pleaded benefit of the clergy.

Rustington, 1571. On about 3 am. 8th May, when Joan, wife of Richard Baker, was lying in bed with her husband, in his dwelling house, she went surreptitiously from the bed, leaving her husband in it. and putting on only her chemise, to a 'draw well', in the garden, feloniously threw herself into it, and drowned in the water, dying immediately.

Shipley, 1571. On 19th July, Maud late wife of Walter Cockles, who was insane and was for that reason bound by her shin with an 'iron plough chain', to a post in her husbands dwelling house. Because of her insanity, feloniously set fire to the house and herself with a burning candle which she held in both hands, and so burned herself to death.

Beckley, 1571. About 6 am on 23rd July, when Robert Morfote, aged over 5, was in bed with another boy in Thomas Glide's house. He got up and went from the room in which he was lying, into an old privy or latrine near the room and, as he stood in the privy on a board which was decayed, the board broke under his weight and by misadventure he fell into the privy to a depth of 9 feet, from which fall and resulting injury he languished until about noon, and then died.

Hollington, 1572. On 1st Dec. Fortune Lucke, aged about 9, a maid servant of Richard Kyte, was sent by Kyte's wife to James Hunt's house, and having the heel and toe of one foot putrefied, she rested in the road, and seized with cold, died a natural death there.

Richard Geeringe died in 1586, aged fifty three, and his eldest son Richard, who was born in 1562, inherited the farm and property. In 1589 he married Grace and became even more prosperous. He also appears to have been a very popular young man. He became a great friend of two of the biggest landowners in that part of Sussex.

They were, Henry Shelley of Patcham Place, who was an ancestor of Percy Bysshe Shelley, the poet. Patcham Place is now a youth hostel, years ago when I belonged to a rambling club, we stayed there, little did I know it had any connection with my ancestors.

Anthony Shirley, seems to have been his best friend, he was the owner of Preston Manor, which had been in his family for a long time, they also owned Wiston Manor about twenty miles away. Anthony Shirley kept about 2,000 sheep at Preston. In 1569, He inherited the Manor, and in 1575, he married Barbara, the daughter of Sir. Thomas Walshingham, and they had twelve

Preston village, the Manor is on the left. The road in the foregound is now the busy London to Brighton road, the A23.

Patcham Place.

children. Anthony and Richard Geeringe were recusants, they refused to attend Church of England services, which was against the law. As they were neighbours, they must have had many private religious discussions in each other's houses, behind closed doors.

By now Richard and Grace had three children, Richard, born in 1589, Thomas in 1592 and Mary in 1594. Sadly, in 1598, Richard died, he was only 36, and his wife Grace was pregnant at the time. He left a Will which reads as follows:

Last Will and Testament of Richard Geeringe
1562 – 1598

In the name of God Amen, I Richard Geeringe of Brightlesmeston (Brighton) in the County of Sussex, this Seventeenth day of November in the One and Fortieth year of the happy reign of our gracious Queen Elizabeth. Being sick in body but in good and perfect memory, I praise God do ordain and make this my testament and last Will in manner form following. First I bequeath my Soul unto Almighty God my creator, hoping that by the merits of Jesus Christ my Saviour he will receive it into his glorious Kingdom, and my body I commend unto the earth to be buried in a place of Christian burial in a convenient place in the Chancel of the Church of Brightelmeston. Item, I give unto the poor people of the said Parish, Twenty Shillings, to be paid by my executors unto the overseers for the poor, within one month next after my decease. Item, I give and bequeath unto Richard Geeringe my eldest son, all my half part of the Prebend of Exceat within the County aforesaid, with all such Scripts, writings and moneyments as I have covering the same, with all tithes, tenth portions, profits, commodities and advantages, my said part belonging or in anywise appertaining; Item I Will and bequeath unto Thomas Geeringe my youngest son, my Windmill standing by the west of the town of Brightelmeston with the ground and appearances thereto belonging. Item I Will and give unto the child with my wife now goeth by, (if it be a son) all my lands, tenements, hereditamnts, Windmill and appurtenances in Withdean within the Parish of Patcham in the County aforesaid. But if it be a daughter, then I do appoint and Will that my next heir unto the premises shall pay unto her forty pounds of lawful money of England, when she shall come to the age of twenty years. Item, I give and bequeath unto my daughter Mary another forty pounds of lawful English money to be paid unto her at twenty years of her age. Item, I give unto Stephen my manservant three shilling and fourpence. Item, I give unto my maid servant Sara Piper, Twenty Pence Items I give unto the poor people of Patcham Twenty shillings to be paid within two months next after my decease.

The residue of all my goods, chattels, and Debts where or what so ever they be. I give unto Grace my wife, whom I do ordain and make my whole and sole executrix. And I do Will and appoint unto the said Grace the manage and bringing up of all my sons and the use and profits of their lands, tenements and all other their portions before bequeathed, until they shall come to the several ages of one and twenty years. And also the keeping of my daughters and use of their portions until the times before to them limited.

And I desire and humbly entreat my good friend the Worshipful Mr. Anthony Sherly of Preston, Esquire and Mr. Henry Shelley of Patcham, Esquire, and Walter Double of Falmer, Yeoman, to be my overseers. And that they will be vouchsafe to be aiding and assisting my said Executor in the guiding, placing and governing of my children, and performing my legacy according to this my testament to the more comfort and quietness of them And to the glory of God to whom be all praise honour and glory now & ever. Amen. And thus have I finished my last Will and confirmed it with my Hand and Seal, the day and year above, said by me Richard Geeringe, resigned and sealed in the presence of William Cartwright, writer hereof. Roger Hewer, Henry Blaker, Robert Geeringe, Richard Cobby and Henry Holland whose signs here appear. (His wife Grace gave birth to a son John in 1598) Probated 6th March 1598

I also have the Wills of two of the wives of Geeringe men, which make quite interesting reading. The first is for Margaret Geeringe who died in 1605, and reads as follows:

"In the name of God Amen. This is the Will nuncupative of Margaret Geeringe widdow, late of the parish of Patcham, within the diocese of Chichester. Deceased, which she pronounced and declared being sick in body but good in perfect memory, on 22nd. day of July Anno Dom. 1605, in manner and form following.

First she willed and bequeathed unto Mary Geeringe, her daughter, Twenty pounds of lawful money of England, one bedstead one bed and all the clothes belonging to it, two chests, six pairs of sheets, one brass pan, two ewe sheep and two whether sheep. She willed and bequeathed to Anne Dumbrell the wife of John Dumbrell, one pair of sheets and six towells and a kettle. She willed and bequeathed unto the said Anne Dumbrell and the aforesaid Mary Geeringe, to either of them three pieces of pewter and one candle stick to each of them a tub and chair. She willed and bequeathed unto Ellinor Rawkins the daughter of Edward Rawkins, her best red petticoat, one ewe and one lamb. To Elizabeth Hobbs the wife of Thomas Hobbs, a russet petticoat. To Margaret Myles a red petticoat, The rest of her wearing clothes she willed and bequeathed to her two daughters.

And the residue of all her goods she willed and bequeathed unto. Thomas her son whom she ordained her sole executor.

And thus she pronounced and finished her last Will and Testament, in the presence of Thomas Rawkins the elder, Thomas Rawkins the younger, and Jo Dumbrell and Elizabeth Hobbs, the day and year above mentioned."

The other Will is for Agnes Geeringe who died in 1616, and reads as follows:

"In the name of God Amen. I Agnes Geeringe, being sick in body but sound in mind, God be thanked. I do make my last Will and Testament as following

I Will and bequeath my three sons William, John and Thomas Geeringe, Forty shillings a piece of good lawful money of England, to be paid unto them twelve months after my decease. I give John Inskipp, Ten shillings, Thomas Inskipp the younger five shillings. Richard Inskipp five shilling

I give Agnes Geeringe daughter of John Geering two best petticoats. I give my best gown to my son John's wife. I give unto the children of my son, ten shillings. I give a pair of pillow cases, to my son William. I give unto my son John a pair of pillow cases. I give unto the said Will and John, two pewter dishes and a platter each. I give the said William and John a chest each. I give the said William and John an iron stool each but John must have the choice. Further it is my Will that my son Thomas should be executor to this my last Will and Testament, and this my executor is to pay these legacies of money unto the above named upon condition that the said William Geeringe do pay unto Thomas my executor, seven pounds and ten shillings of good and lawful money of England within twelve months after my decease. Or if this debt be not acknowledged or paid by the said William unto Thomas Geeringe, then none shall have power or licence to ask or demand any legacy of money of the said Thomas my executor.

I give John Inskipp a good sheet. Dated the thirteen day of April Anno Dom.1616.

I do ordain that John Osbourne and Richard Smyth should be overseers of Will, and that they should see my Will performed.

I give an "Edward", twelve pence unto Elizabeth Smyth."

Grace, the widow of Richard was thirty two, and soon after her husband's death, she gave birth to a son John. She now had four young children the eldest Richard was only nine years old, but of course she was well provided for, also Anthony Shirley, who had been the main overseer of her husbands Will, remained a good friend of the family, and helped in any way he could.

In 1600, Grace married another Yeoman from Poynings,

close by. His name was William Pryor, he was a single man, and there were no children from this marriage. He probably helped her to manage the property left to the children until they came of age.

Richard, the eldest son married Mary Simmons in 1607, he was Eighteen, in 1610, he came of age, and inherited the estate. In 1613, his mother died, she was Forty Two. Three months later, her Second husband William Pryor died. Her daughter Mary was Nineteen, and was the chief beneficiary of William Pryor's Will, I suppose he thought the boys had been well provided for. Thomas was now Twenty One and in 1614, married Ann Midhurst. John was Sixteen.

In the 'Abstracts of Sussex Deeds', there is an entry dated 17th.0ct. 1618, which

"Lease by Richard Geering, Yeoman, to William Thomas of Lewes, gent, of his moiety of the Prebend of Exceat for Twenty years at a yearly rent of Twenty Pounds to be paid at the dwelling house of William Foster scrivener in Lewes."

In 1620, Richard Geering, gent, acts as a surety, at the marriage of Henry Shirley of Preston, gent, and Mary Seaman of Glynde, widow. Henry was the son of Anthony Shirley of Preston Manor, he died in 1630. We also find that in 1630, Richard Geering becomes the Bailiff of Preston which is quite an important position, which he holds – until 1650.

We now come to the youngest son John, from whom my family are descended. In 1619, he was Twenty One and would have inherited the land and Windmill left to him by his father at Withdean. John never knew his father, but would have known about him being a dissenter, in spite of having been buried in the Chancel of the Parish Church of Brighton, which was usually reserved for important people. He would have also known about the turbulent times of Henry VIII, when he dissolved the Monasteries and brought about the reformation, and people being put to death for their religious beliefs, by Queen Mary.

By the beginning of the seventeenth century, when John was

growing up, many religious sects were forming, such as the Lutherans, the Calvinistic Presbyterians, Quakers and Baptists. All of these sects were illegal and their followers were still being persecuted, many of them set sail for the New World, America, in the wake of the Pilgrim Fathers. A few Baptists communities were springing up in Sussex, and there was a thriving community in Ditchling, just the other side of the Downs from Patcham. John married a girl from a Baptist family, her name was Margaret Looker, and she came from Ditchling, and that is where they were married and set up home in 1627.

The communities in Sussex, belonged to a group of dissenters called General Baptists and their story began early in the reign of James I. A number of English dissenters led by Browne and Robinson had, in 1581, fled to Holland to escape the attention of the notorious Archbishop Whitgift, who in the reign of Queen Elizabeth I had had Barrow and Greenwood executed in 1593 at Tyburn. They were followed by others fleeing persecution, John Smyth and Thomas Helwys, after the accession of James I, could see no lessening of the persecution of dissenters, and also fled to Holland. Robinson was to lead the Pilgrim Fathers to a new life in America in 1620, but Helwys and his followers became increasingly uneasy with the desertion of English dissent, and in 1612 they returned to England and commenced to worship in Spitalfields, London. In Holland, convinced that the New Testament taught the baptism of believers, Smyth had rebaptised himself, and then Helwys and others.

The Spitafields company became the first Baptist Church in England. Helwys was soon thrown into Newgate prison on account of his demands for religious liberty, where subsequently died four years later. How the dissenters fared in the reign of Charles I and his cruel Primate Archbishop Laud cannot be told in detail.

Because the early Baptists took seriously their duty to pass on their faith, groups of believers were to be found during the early years of the 17th.Century, in Kent, Sussex, and the other Home Counties. Their characteristics, which lasted well into the 18th.Century.

In the reign of Charles II several Acts of Parliament placed - severe restrictions on dissenters and resulted in much persecution and hardship. In 1662 and 1664 acts were passed, by which all religious assemblies of five or more persons other then the people of the house were made illegal, and subject to a penalty of £20. on each person, or imprisonment if not paid. Many tales of repression and heroism are recorded for this era, the story of John Bunyan probably the best known.

Most of the Baptists were educated Yeomen and met secretly in each others barns. By the reign of William and Mary, the 1689 Toleration Act ended active persecution and dissenters were tolerated, but required a licence for all meeting places.

John and Margaret had twelve children, eight boys and four girls, the last child to be born was a son, who they named Henry, born in 1642, and was to become my ancestor. There wouldn't have been much for Henry to inherit, but he seems to have managed alright, like his brothers and sisters was brought up as a Baptist.

In 1673, at the age of Thirty One, Henry married Elizabeth Holden, also a Baptist, they had four children. The eldest son was called Henry like his father, he was born in 1683 in the village of Clayton, which is about Two miles from Ditchling, I think his father was a small holder, as he paid tithes as property owner.

When young Henry was Twenty Two, in 1705, he married Mary Berry from the nearby village of Wivelsfield. I don't know what he did for a living, but they lived in Keymer, which is between Clayton and Ditchling.

Their first son was another Henry born in 1707, in Keymer, the family were still Baptists. I think the family were still small holders and sheep farmers, because they all paid tithes on their properties.

When this Henry grew up he married a young lady named

Sarah, I do not know her surname, as there is no record of their marriage in any of the local Church records. It was quite common for non-conformists to be married by an un-ordained minister, outside the Church, which was of course illegal. Henry and Sarah were very strict Baptists, so they would have had the ceremony Blessed in about 1728, as their first child was born in 1729, followed by eight more, the last of which was born in 1765, some time after that Sarah died, and Henry married another Sarah, she was a widow named Buchman, her maiden name was Caffin. There were no children from this marriage, the 2nd Sarah was also a very strict Baptist. Her father was the Baptist minister at Horsham.

In 1727, an Act was passed allowing non-conformists to practice their religions by building Chapels and Meeting Houses. Henry and Sarah, got together with others in their community at Ditchling, and they built a Meeting House there, which is still used. In the Will of William Caffin, Sarah's uncle, and dated 1767, he made Henry Gearing of Ditchling his joint executor, and Henry Gearing and his wife, with others, joint residual beneficiaries. Also when the father of Sarah died in 1778 she was a beneficiary of his Will. Henry die,d in 1785.

One of the children of his first marriage was William, he was actually born at Bolney, about Ten miles north of Clayton, I

Ditchling Meeting House.

Clayton Parish Church.

don't know what they were doing there as all the other children were born in Clayton. In 1769 William married a girl from a well to do Sussex family, her name was Ann Friend. I don't know what William did for a living, but he paid tithes on a house "In Clayton Woods", which was between Clayton and Keymer and is less than a mile from Ditchling, so they were not too far from the Meeting House around which their social life seemed to have revolved. William and Ann had four children, two boys and two girls, the eldest of whom was Henry. He was born in 1770, and Christened in the lovely old Saxon Church of St. John the Baptist at Clayton. His father, was a very great friend of the lay minister at the Meeting House, his name was John Burgess, who kept a shop in Ditchling, he was a craftsman and trader, and called himself a glover, his skills with leather required him to make soft leather into garments such as trousers and coats, working gloves, and special gloves for church, funerals, and the like. Thus he had learned the skills of the fellmonger to prepare the skins of sheep and deer. He also kept a daily "Jernal" from 1785 to 1790, in which he often mentioned the Gearing's.

His descendant, Don Burgess has transcribed the 'Jernal', and published it, the original is in the East Sussex Record Office. In the Preface of the Diary, the transcriber has written "His spelling was sometimes phonetic, as one would expect from an age where there was no general and standard education for literacy, and books and newspapers were more scarce than today. However his accuracy in writing of places and people has been found very reliable, and useful for research purposes". The following extracts are the entries which refer to William Gearing and his son Henry:

Mon. 11th Apri 1785. Work in ye shop in ye forenoon and in ye afternoon went to Franklins to see Mas. Burne because he was going to Billinhurst to live that nix day stopd there all ye afternoon helping load the goods Brother Billinghurst was loader etc. Mr. Gearing & I came home together about 10 oclock.

Sun. 8th May. Was at home it was our full meeting day Mr. Evershed was hear received in 2 members Namely Geering & Judge. (I think that would have been Henry Gearing, aged 15).

Tu. 26 July 1785. Went to mending the old Barn got Mr. Gearing to help.

Sat. 6 August. Repairing ye yard &c. with Mas. Gearing.

Sat 30 Jul. this forenoon Mr. Gearing & I was fiting up my yard after noon work in ye shop

Sat. 6 Aug. 1785, repairing ye yard &c. with Mas, Geering.

Wed 21 Sept. 1785. Went to Wealbridge Common with master Geering to help him repair his House stopd half day came home about one oclock had some loose wheat threshed by mas Fryer 2 Bushels.

Here are some entries which do not include the Geering's but are quite interesting:

25th. Sep. 1785 A sermon was preached by Mr. Eversheed the remains of the time was spent in disciplin after service we went down to Mr.Vines had some dinner there was some provided for a few that came from afar we had a large mutton pye & apple & damson pye all cold for dinner etc.

Sat. 29th. Oct. 1785. Great deal of snow fell this morning we have had some snow a few days before this year & some sharp frosts. (October').

Tu. 8th. Nov. Helping the Carpenters at ye yard etc. Father Edward & Richard was here at dinner we had rosted Goose.

Wed. 23 Dec. 1785. Went to Mr. Chatfields at Rookery to dinner with father Edwards about 2 oclock had good piece of boyled Beef & I rost Duck and plum pudden for dinner after dinner we had a pot of good punch & smokd a pipe.

Th. 2nd. Mar. 1786. Work in ye yard amaking & putting up wring Master Geering was helping me.

Tu. 8th. Aug. 1786. father fell from a horse. We had Rost Beef for dinner apple & bread pudden.

Wed. 16th. Aug. 1786 Was wringing some tan leather great part of ye day got Master Geering to help turn for me.

Fri. 22nd. Aug. this morning went to Rookery took my mony for reeping one acre & half weat in Brooms Croat ar 8/- acre. Mas Geering & I reeped it between us we had no bite nor beer all the time.

Mu. 4th. Dec. 1786. Went to Lewes Sitting to pay my duty which was 0.4.31/2 rode Mr. Welches horse & carried his duty which was 3-5-0 Cared a piece of Linsuey to Mr. Joneses to ye fulling mill for Mr. Geering. Went to ye Crown Lewes to see a very remarkable Ox that was there for a show it was like other Oxen in every respect except it's head and that had only one Horne Growed Strait out of its poul about 3 feet 8 inches or near 4 feet round & was so long as to prevent his grasing So that he Cant get his mouth to ye ground so that he is oblidge to be fed with bran &c in a different manner he is about 5 years old breiad in Scotland Gave 2d to see him – his Horne Spreed So wide that it nearly Covered one of his eyes – he is a very large well mad of a ridish caller &c. Caled at Mr. Martens got womens great coat home for Mrs. Welch gave 1 = 1 = 0 for it &c. Went to Mr. Kennards Bot 71b Ginger bread.

Wed. 26th. Dec 1786 Went to Mr. Drawbridges Linfield to dinner we had ledg mutten & Bread pudden for dinner I stopd till about 7 oclock we had some comfortable Conversation upon morral & religious subjects.

Wed. 20th. June 1787 Went to Brighthelmstone after a let-pass to Carry 2 packs Wool to Lewes to Mr. Chatfield &c. I bought 7 Mackril for 6d. & Quart of Rigrels for 2d. Went packing wool after I came home had mas Geering to help me.

Mon. 30th. July 1787 Work building Hog pound Mr. Geering helping me.

Tue. 7th. Aug. 1787 this morning went to Lewes Heard Several Law Suites tryed & heard Great part of Philip Ginden tryal he was convicted of ye wilful Murder of a person at Preston Ginden was an officer of ye Excise ye deceased was a smugler they met upon the sea beach a large body of Smuglers & Ginden 3 other men made a large seasyer the deceased received a large cut upon the head with a broad surd another man was very much cut. Ginden was ye first man I have ever see condmnd to be hanged he did not seem to be much effected at his Sentence &c.

Wed. 29th. Aug. This afternoon Mas Geering & I Reepd about 1 acre & quartes we had 14/- Between us for reeping of it no Bait (bite) &c.

Tue. 25th. Dec. Was at home Smith preached upon Luke 2=10=11. We had a piece of Beef Boild for dinner allott of about 1 stone Sent as a present by a person unknown.

Fri. 14th. Mar. Went to Fryars Oake (a pub.) to a Bull Bait to sell my dog I sold him for 1 Guineay upon condition he was hurt but as he recvd no hurt I took him again at the same price I had all my Expences paid because I had a dog there was 5 or 6 dogs but mine was Called the best. We had a good dinner a round of Beef Boild A good piece of roasted a Lag of mutten & Ham of pork & plum pudden plenty of wine & punch all the after noon there was a great many people.

Mu. 26th. May 1788. Was carrying mould out of ye Garden mas Geering & I began to dig a Draw Well in ye garden for ye use of ye yard &c. we only got about 6 feet deep to day &c.

Sun. llth. June 1788. Went to Lewes Meeting Went to Mr. Lampiers to dinner had rost Veal & Gusbury pudden.

Sat. 3rd. Jan 1789. Helping mas Geering Scour out his Well in the evening went

Fri. 30th. Jan. 1789. We have had a remarkable Sharp Frost Great deal of Snow likewise the frost began 24th Nov.1788 & lasted about 8 weeks many poeple say it more severe Cold then it was in the hard Winter Water was scarce and very bad many wells dry has been so very dry for so long time Great Numbers of fish perished as Well as Birds &c.

The diary closed on 14th. February 1790. Master Henry Geering, was fifteen, when Mr. John Burgess started the journal, and young Henry was apprenticed to a Tallow Chandler, tallow was made from animal fat, and was used to make candles, soap and grease. As John Burgess dealt in leather, it was probably good work experience for Henry.

In 1795, at the age of Twenty Five, he decided to leave home, and moved to Greenwich. I don't know what his reasons were, because he had a good job, and his parents were not poor, although, the Industrial Revolution had started, and many people were leaving the land to move to the cities.

I believe he came to Greenwich by boat, as the roads in

Sussex were very bad, and there was a boat service from Shoreham, stopping at Brighton, Hastings, Dover, Gravesend and finally Greenwich.

CHAPTER TWO

GREENWICH 1795 – 1821

Henry set himself up as a tallow chandler, somewhere by the river at Crane Street or Highbridge, to be near the sailing ships and barges, as they used a lot of tallow, also there was a big cattle market at Deptford.

I have an 1820's print taken from the river, on the east side of the Naval College. It shows a small building, with a taller one next to it, on the site where the Trafalgar Tavern now stands, it may have been the Yacht Tavern. The Trafalgar Tavern was not built until 1835.

Next to these buildings, is a wooden landing stage, jutting out, with a couple of children playing on it, and a fisherman sitting on a box, mending his nets, talking to another fisherman, in a rowing boat with nets hanging over the side. In the corner against the wall, where the walkway starts going round the front of the Naval College, there is a flight of steps going down to the river, which seems to be a picking up point for passengers to board boats rowed by watermen, who were the river taxi men and were called wherrymen. The Thames was full of them, as most people travelled by water, there was no public transport, and only the rich could afford carriages. Also there was only one bridge, which was London Bridge.

In this print there are three boats with passengers in them,

1820'S print taken from the river from the east.

and some more descending the steps to board a waiting boat which were called wherries.

Going eastwards along the river front along Crane Street to Highbridge, there were probably more old buildings overlooking the river and boat sheds, Henry Gearing may have had his tallow chandler's premises in one of the sheds. At the end of Highbridge, was the Crown and Sceptre public house, which was built in the eighteenth century.

I have another print dated 1796 of Highbridge Wharfe, where Trinity Hospital is situated in the middle of the picture, it stands well back from the river. To the eastern side of it is a long building, which was Crowley House, built in the reign of Charles I, by a city merchant and later occupied by an M.P. Gregory Clemont. He was thrown out of Parliament for misbehaviour with serving maid at Greenwich. During the reign of Charles II. it was owned by George Bowerman, who obtained an order to ballast the King's Ships, which he did from Ballast Quay. The House was pulled down in the nineteenth century,

Crown and Sceptre Tavern.

Highbridge Wharfe, showing Trinity Hospital, centre, and Crowley House, left, and the Crown and Sceptre Tavern on the right..

and Greenwich Power Station now occupies the site. Ballast Quay is still there, but at that time there were no buildings on it. In 1815 the Union Tavern and the houses on the east side of it were built. The pub is now called the 'The Cutty Sark'.

Beyond Ballast Quay there were no roads or buildings, just the Greenwich Marshes which stretched halfway up towards Old Woolwich Road, which in those days, was the main highway running through East Greenwich, from Park Row. Where Trafalgar Road is now, was all wooded, you can tell by the names of the roads, such as Woodlands Crescent, Woodlands Walk and Woodlands Park Road. It was all part of the park of about fifty acres surrounding Westcombe Manor House, which stood where Peacham Road is, off Humber Road. It was built in 1723, and owned by Sir. Gregory Page, who lived in a huge mansion, called Wricklemarsh at Lee he let Westcombe to various tenants. About a mile to the east of it, was Woodlands House, owned by John Julius Angerstein, whose estate stretched down to the river as did the park surrounding Charlton Manor.

Vanbrugh Hill was called Love Lane or Green Lane. Blackwall Lane was called Marsh Lane, right up until Blackwall Tunnel was opened by Queen Victoria in 1897, my father sat on his father's shoulders to watch the ceremony, my grandfather always called it Marsh Lane.

At the top end of Marsh Lane there were a few cottages and small farms. On the main road going towards Charlton there were a few more cottages, beyond which it was all farm land and market gardens going all the way to Woolwich. Henry Gearing's father died in 1796 in Sussex, and in 1797 Henry married Elizabeth Nicholls at St. Nicholas Church, Deptford. Their first born son Henry, was born in 1798, at Greenwich, followed by a second son Thomas in 1802 and three more girls born later.

In 1810, at the age of twelve, young Henry joined the Navy. It was quite common in those days for boys to go to sea at that age. I don't know if he ran away from home, or joined with his parents consent. Nelson, the Nations hero, had died at the

31

'Battle of Trafalgar', five years earlier in 1805. It is quite possible that young Henry was taken by his father to the Painted Hall in Greenwich Hospital, to see the 'Lying-in-State', of Lord Nelson, which may have influenced him.

Henry senior's mother died in Sussex in 1812, she was Seventy. In her will she left him forty pounds, and a similar legacy to her two married daughters in Sussex and a smaller amount to their children. Unfortunately her other son John had died leaving a young widow and daughter Mary Anne. To this daughter she left the sum of one hundred pounds when she attained the age of twenty one. She also set up a trust fund for her maintenance and education. After other bequests, the residue of her estate was to be equally divided between Henry and his sisters, also if Mary Anne died before she was twenty one, her legacy was to be divided between them.

Young Henry left the Navy, after serving for four years in 1814, he was sixteen and his father then apprenticed him as a Waterman and Lighterman on the River Thames, it was the year the Thames froze over.

Frozen Thames, 1814.

I still have his original indentures, and quote from them as follows:

"THIS INDENTURE – Witnesseth, That Henry Gearing, Son of Henry Gearing, of the Parish of St. Alphage, Greenwich, in the County of Kent, doth put himself, Apprentice to Thomas Starkey, of the Parish aforesaid. In the County aforesaid. WATERMAN AND LIGHTER-MAN."

"To learn his art, and with him after the manner of an Apprentice to dwell and serve upon the River Thames, from the day of the date here-of, until the full end and term of seven years from thence next following, to be fully complete and ended, during which term, the said apprentice his said Master faithfully shall serve. His secrets keep, his lawful command-ments everywhere gladly do. He shall do no damage to his said Master, nor see it be done by others, but he in his power, shall let or forthwith give warning to his said Master of the same; He shall not waste the goods of the said Master, nor lend them unlawfully to any. He shall not commit fornication, nor con-tract matrimony within the said term. He shall not play cards, dice, tables or any unlawful games, whereby his said Master may have any loss. With his own goods or others during the said term, without licence of his said Master, he shall not buy nor sell; He shall not haunt taverns or playhouses, nor absent himself from his Masters service day or night, unlawfully, but in all things as a faithful Apprentice he shall behave himself towards his said master, during the said term. And the said Master in consideration of services of his said apprentice in the same art which he useth by the best means that he can, shall teach and instruct or cause to be taught and instructed, finding unto the said apprentice meat, drink, apparel, lodging and all other necessaries, according to the custom of the City of London.

In witness whereof, the parties above named to these indentures, have put their hands and seals. The Twenty Fourth Day of October 1814. Signed and sealed in the presence of: Henry Gearing and Thomas Starkey."

After finishing their apprenticeship, they were examined by the Master and Wardens of the 'Company of Watermen and Lightermen,' at Watermen's Hall, in the City of London. If found to be satisfactory, they became Freemen of the Company and River Thames, and could take any commercial craft up to Fifty Tons, up or down the River.

The Watermen who ferried the passengers in small boats, only served a two year apprenticeship. The origin of the 'Company of Watermen and Lightermen', go back to 1514, when Parliament found it necessary to introduce some form of control, of the many men who earned a living on the river. An act was passed to regulate fares on the Thames.

The watermen, however, continued to act independently, and act of 1555 appointed Rulers of all watermen and wherry-men, working between Gravesend and Windsor, and thus the Company was born.

The act of 1555 also introduced apprenticeship for a term of one year for all boys wishing to learn the watermen's trade, this was extended to seven years in 1603 by a further act.

In 1700 the lightermen, who hitherto had been members of the Woodmongers' Company, succeeded in their petitions to Parliament, and an Act of that year brought them into the Watermen's Company. From then on lightermen were bound by the same regulations as applied to watermen and in suc-ceeding years their numbers grew with the trade of the Port of London, while those of the watermen diminished with the improvement of road transport in the Cities of London and Westminster.

An Act of 1827 was important in that for the first time the Company became completely independent and a body corpo-rate with it's own seal. At an early stage in its life the Company achieved two marks of distinction. In 1585 Arms were granted by Queen Elizabeth and, before the end of the century, the

Company possessed a Hall.

Doggett's Coat and Badge: This ancient sculling race tradi-
tionally is only open to apprentices who have completed their
apprenticeship and taken up the Freedom of the Company
within twelve months preceding the day of the race. The course
from London Bridge to Chelsea is a furlong short of five miles,
and the prize of the orange redcoat and silver badge is much
treasured by freemen of the Company. The 'wager' has been
rowed every year since its inception in 1715. Thomas Doggett,
the Irish comedian who founded it to celebrate the anniversary
of the accession of the House of Hanover to the throne of
England.

Royal Watermen to the Monarch are shrouded in time.
Today, licensed Thames Watermen wishing to become Royal
Watermen have to apply to the Lord Chamberlain offering their
services to the Monarch, and after often many years of waiting,
they will be short listed and following security checks, will be
invited to the Palace for an interview. Those successful will be
appointed to replace retiring men. The number is maintained at
Twentythree active appointments.

The Queen's Watermen today, perform a mainly ceremonial
role. They no longer row the Monarch, as today's Royal Barge
is a motor powered vessel, the 'Royal Nore'.

One of the duties of the Royal Watermen, is delivering the
Crown and State Regalia to The Palace of Westminster for the
State Opening of Parliament. The Crown procession leaves
Buckingham Palace ahead of the Queen's procession. The
Crown used to be rowed down river from Hampton Court, it
being displayed in the Barge for the citizens to see.

The Company also maintain several charities by providing
Homes for elderly lightermen and their wives, there is one at
Penge, and two in Sussex, one in Hastings and another in
Ditchling.

From time immemorial until well after the Battle of
Trafalgar, the Thames was the richest source of manpower for
Britain's Navy, many of whom were press ganged into it.

Her Majesty's Barge Master Bob Crouch. He was also an ex Master of the Company of Watermen.

Delivering the Crown to the Palace of Westminster.

Bob Crouch with other Royal bargemen.

For over four centuries, son has followed father as a Freeman of the Company. It is small wonder, therefore, that the waterman has come to look upon Watermen's Hall with regard and affection as he reflects upon his family's associations with the Company, and it is to be hoped that his support of his ancient Guild will ensure its prosperity for the benefit of future generations.

This is a copy of Henry Gearing's Seaman's Certificate after he left the Navy. Henry Gearing, Born in Greenwich, Kent, on 6th.December 1798.

'Marks; none. Hair; Dark Brown. Eyes; blue. Can write; Yes. Went to sea as an apprentice in the year 1810. Has served in the Royal Navy, Four Years.'

The other son, Thomas, was apprenticed to a shoe maker, after serving his apprenticeship, he became a master shoemaker, and had his workshop in Park Street Greenwich. On the 1851, census, his occupation is given as 'Shoemaker for Greenwich Hospital School.' Having been educated at Greenwich Hospital School, which was re-named 'The Royal Hospital School' in the latter half of the nineteenth century. I know quite a bit about the history of the school and Greenwich Hospital. For those who do not know it's history, I had better start from the beginning:

The old royal Palace of Greenwich, was built in the reign of the Tudors, at the beginning of the 16th century, and called 'The Palace of Placentia' Both Henry VIII and Queen Elizabeth I. were born and held their Courts there. When Elizabeth died in 1603, and King James, came to the throne he did not want to live there, and held his courts in St. James' Palace. Gradually the old Palace at Greenwich fell into disrepair.

When William and Mary, came to the throne in 1685, Queen Mary decided she would like to build a Hospital for Naval Pensioners, similar to the one Nell Gwynne had built for Old Soldiers, at Chelsea. The old royal palace at Greenwich was

The old royal Palace of Greenwich, which was called 'The Palace of Placentia'.

pulled down, and Queen Mary commissioned Sir Christopher Wren, to build a magnificent hospital for her gallant sailors, in 1694. In those days a hospital did not have the same meaning as it does today, any home or hostel, for the poor, old or disabled was called a hospital. The reason I mention this, is because, many of the so-called pensioners, were not old men, but young sailor's who had lost a limb or were disabled, also men left the navy at a much earlier age, as Henry Gearing did, although he did not live there he was classified as a naval pensioner at sixteen years of age!

When the Hospital was finally completed, a lot of them were married or wanted to marry, but their wives had to live out, usually in Greenwich.

By the early 18th century, the Queen's House opposite, was not being used so the commissioners of the charity which had been set up by Queen Mary, decided to turn it into an asylum or school in 1712, for the education of the children of naval pensioners, and the first head master was the Astronomer Royal. Sadly, the Queen did not live long enough to see her project

Greenwich Hospital.

completed, but King William continued with it, and set up the charity to last into perpetuity. Financed from the income the property the royal family owned in Greenwich, and some big estates in the north of England and Scotland, which had been owned by Nobles, who had been executed for treason, and their property confiscated by the crown.

This description of the Hospitals was taken from the National Directory for Kent, in 1839.

"In describing the public edifices, the Hospital, that unrivalled monument of Christian benevolence and national gratitude and munificence, is pre-eminently entitled to precedence. It is a noble stone building, founded by William and Mary in 1694 – seated on the bank of the Thames, on an elevated terrace, about eight hundred and sixty five feet in length towards the river; it consist of four distinct structures, distinguished by the names of King Charles, Queen Anne's, King William's and Queen Mary's the interval between the two most northern buildings forms the grand square, which is upwards of two hundred and seventy feet in width. In one of these piles is a chapel which, for neatness, elegance and real beauty, is not surpassed by any sanctuary in the kingdom; an eminent connoisseur thus speaks of it; "for truly classical design, in which no ornament is applied but from antique example, the chapel of Greenwich Hospital, as restored by the Athenian Stuart, has no rival in England. The painted hall, governor's hall, the several offices &c., have been similarly eulogised. From its position immediately opposite to an d on the margin of the Thames, the prospect from the hospital is of the most delightful character, commanding the expansive course of this far famed river, with vessels in continual motion on its ample bosom, and embracing an extensive line of the coast of Essex. To do justice to the beauty of this universally celebrated institution, in a work necessarily limited as this is, would be impossible – indeed it must be seen to be properly appreciated; and, as an attempt at further description would be utterly futile, we must reluctantly decline the task. To the south of the hospital is the Naval Asylum, or school for the education, maintenance and clothing of children of seamen and marines; this is an extensive and truly liberal institution, and comprises Every requisite office upon a scale uniformly grand – including large school rooms, refectory, dormitory, an elegant chapel, infirmary, &c. encompassed by pleasant grounds, lawns and gardens. These are the charities of great magnitude.

ROYAL HOSPITAL
NAVAL DEPARTMENT

Governor – Rear Admiral Sir. Thomas M. Hardy Bart. G.C.B.
Lieut. Governor – Rear Admiral Sir Jahleel Brenton, Bart. K.C.B.
Captains. – William Edge, Robert Larkan, Thos. Huskisson, D. Woodriff. C.B.
Lieuts – F. Bedford, W. Renwick, W. Rivers, N. Tucker, W. Tosper, M. Fitron Edward de Montmorency and John Wood Rouse.

UPPER SCHOOL

Superintending Captain – Thomas Huskisson R.N.
Lieutenant – William Tosper.
Chaplain & Headmaster – Rev. George Fisher.
Mathematical Teacher – Edward Riddle, R.N.

LOWER SCHOOL
Master – Rev. S. Gallon
Assistant – W. Passingham

Edward Riddle became a famous mathematician, and wrote several books on the subject.

Rear Admiral Sir. Thomas Hardy, had served under Lord Nelson, and was with him when he died.

By 1869 very few pensioners were in residence, and the hospital was closed, and in 1873 The Greenwich Hospital Charity, leased it to the Royal Navy and it became the Royal Naval College. It is now leased to Greenwich University.

CHAPTER THREE

GREENWICH 1821 – 1844

In 1821, young Henry married Elizabeth Humphreys at St. Nicholas Church, Deptford. He was twenty three years old and she was twenty two, and had been born in Gosport, but had moved to Deptford with her family, as her brother was a witness at their marriage.

Henry was still apprenticed but was not yet a Freeman of the Company of Watermen and Lightermen. However, as he had served seven years of his apprenticeship, he would have been allowed to marry.

In fact he did not become a Freeman until 1824. I do not know why it took so long. Maybe it was because his master had assigned him over to another master, William Frewin in 1816, which may have caused the delay, or he may have been a slow learner, there was a lot to be learnt in navigating such a busy river, with its treacherous currents. He would have had to be able to skipper a fully laden Thames sailing barge, and be familiar with all the rigging of the sails etc.

On the 19th June 1823, his new master wrote to the Company, in which he said "Gentlemen, I have no objection to his Freedom." Henry finally became free on 1st. April 1824, and so he had served as an apprentice for ten years with out earning any money.

The result was, their first child was born in Greenwich work house, which was near Royal Hill in West Greenwich. Henry's father had inherited money from his mother, who had died in Sussex a few years earlier. I don't suppose he could help much, as his other son was being apprenticed as a shoemaker, also he had his wife and four other children to support, and times were very hard for everyone at that time.

The Napoleonic wars had recently finished, which had almost bankrupted the country. Hundreds of soldiers and sailors, had returned from the wars and looking for work. Also the Industrial Revolution had begun, and thousands of agricultural workers, were thrown out of work, due to the introduction of threshing machines.

Whole families were flocking to London and other big cities. It was the period Dickens wrote about in 'Oliver Twist', 'David Copperfield', and 'Little Dorrit'.

In the early 1820's the workhouses were packed, many people became destitute, as there was no other alternative if you lost your job. The child was named Henry William, and was christened at St. Alphege church, Greenwich, on 30th June 1822, the father's occupation was given as Mariner N.P. which stood for naval pensioner, even though he was only sixteen when he left the Navy!

His poor wife Elizabeth, remained in the workhouse with the baby, until April 1823, and then from September until December of that year. During this time she was given 2.0s. per week.

THE DAILY DIET IN THE GREENWICH WORK HOUSE, AT THAT TIME WAS:

SUNDAY:	BREAKFAST. One Quart of Milk Pottage. DINNER, Six oz. Beef when cooked and free from the bone, 1lb. Potatoes
MONDAY:	BREAKFAST, One oz. of Butter or two oz. of Cheese.

	DINNER, One Quart of good Soup made from Sunday's dinner.
TUESDAY:	BREAKFAST, One Quart of Rice Milk.
	DINNER: Six oz. Beef, one llb. of Potatoes.
WEDNESDAY:	BREAKFAST, One oz. of Butter or Two oz. of Cheese.
	DINNER: One Quart of good Soup made from Tuesday's dinner.
THURSDAY:	BREAKFAST, One Quart of Milk Pottage.
	DINNER, Six oz. Mutton, One Ib. of Potatoes.
FRIDAY:	BREAKFAST,' One oz. of Butter or two of Cheese.
	DINNER, One Quart of good Soup made from Thursday's dinner.
SATURDAY:	BREAKFAST, One Quart of Rice Milk.
	DINNER, Twelve oz. of Suet Pudding.
SUPPER:	Every Day, Two oz. of Cheese or one oz. of Butter.
CHRISTMAS DAY:	Eight oz. of Cooked or Baked Beef and Vegetables.
	Twelve oz. of Plum Pudding.
	One Pint of Strong Beer.

On two days in the summer, Five oz. of Bacon and Green Peas.
On two other days, Five oz. Bacon and Green Peas.
On four other days. Good Mackerel and One lb. of Potatoes.
On four other days. Good Herring and One lb. of Potatoes.
On six other days. Good salt Fish instead of Meat.

> Each adult and children over twelve years of age were to receive; Fourteen oz. of Bread and Two Pints of Beer per day.

They certainly fared much better in Greenwich, than poor Oliver Twist did!

It appears that the guardians of the poor were also officer's of the parish, and sometimes discussed parochial affairs at the workhouse. On one occasion, it was brought to their notice, that the inhabitants of Blackheath Road, complained to the beadle about boys misbehaving themselves and he was ordered to apprehend persons who shall be guilty of such offence and prosecute accordingly.

On 14th May 1824, they discussed a bill for lighting the towns of Greenwich and Deptford, in the County of Kent, and establishing a Gas Light Company. On 2nd May 1824, a provision of the bill would enable the purchase of a limited number of acres to be used by them for the purpose of the Company, but no restriction was imposed as to the situation of the land. Owners to be compensated by damage in laying the pipes, and the Company to make good the pavements in case of delays.

In 1840, a new workhouse with infirmary attached, was built in a field at the bottom of what was Love Lane and is now known as Vanbrugh Hill.

Up until the Second World War. the workhouse was still in use. There were railings at the front, going along Woolwich Road. I remember as a boy seeing the old men sitting behind them, wearing grey tweed suits and cap. The infirmary was known as St. Alphage Hospital. After the war it was pulled down, to be replaced by Greenwich District Hospital.

By 1825, Henry was working, and they had another child Hannah, followed in 1827 by a son John James, who was to become my great grandfather, and then in 1831, a daughter Caroline, which completed the family. They were then living in East Lane, which was later called Old Woolwich Road.

In 1833, at the age of eleven years, young Henry William, became a pupil at the Greenwich Hospital School, he was able to become a pupil there, as his father had served in the Royal Navy. He was quite a bright lad, and went into the Upper School, which consisted of four hundred boys, the sons of officer's, seamen and mariner's in the Royal service, who received an excellent practical education in navigation and nautical astronomy. The course of education, also embraced religious instruction and ordinary branches of English learning. The first

Greenwich Hospital School in the 1830's.

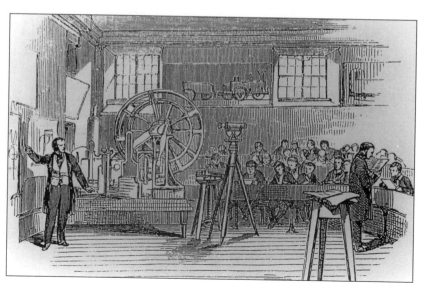

Learning to use a sextant.
Greenwich Hospital School in the 1830's.

Marching to the dining hall.
Greenwich Hospital School in the 1830's.

William Penn's engineering works in 1840.

class extended to geometry, algebra, engineering and steam machinery, chart and mechanical drawing.

After he left school, he may have gone to work at, John Penn & Sons. engine works, in Blackheath Road, Greenwich, which was founded in 1825, making marine steam engines, which they supplied to major shipbuilders throughout the world. He eventually became a ship's engineer, and by the early 1840's was with a Danish shipping line, which traded with India. He used to sail to Calcutta, where he settled in 1844, and married Elizabeth Jane Oliphant, at St. Andew's Church, Calcutta. His bride was the daughter of Capt. George Oliphant, 22nd Native Regiment, Infantry. He had arrived in India in about 1800, as a young ensign, and had been born in Cockspur Street, which was a continuation of Pall Mall, and was christened in St. Margaret's Church, Westminster.

Henry was twenty-three and Elizabeth twenty-two. They had five children born between and 1845 and 1851, but only two survived, Henry George, born in 1845, and William John in

Above left:
L. Henry William Gearing 1822-1860's.

Above right:
Henry George Gearing, 1845-1916, India.

Left:
R. Henry Allen Cheshire Gearing, 1884-1917. He was born in India but died in England whilst serving in the Australian army.

India 1910, marriage of Mary Gearing and Charles D'Arcy Crofton I.C.S. who is standing behind the left shoulder of the bride. Standing far left is Sir Christopher Masterman I.C.S. who married Mary's sister Hope. All the other men in the picture were also in the I.C.S.

Mrs. Henry Gearing seated, with her three daughters and their husbands. India 1920. Left to right: Sir Christopher Masterman, Mary Crofton, Brig. Louis and Dorothy Woodhouse, Charles Crofton, and Hope Masterman.

1850. The others had died in early childhood, which was quite common in India in those days. Sadly their mother Elizabeth died in 1852, aged thirty years, I don't know what became of William, he may have died later or emigrated.

Henry George, became an engineer, and in 1872, married Mary Ann Grinnol at St. Stephen's Church, Kidderpore. They had six children. two boys and four girls, all of whom became part of the Raj in India. One daughter Hope, married Sir. Christopher Masterman, a senior official in the Indian civil service. Another Mary, also married an official in the Indian civil service, Charles D'arcy Crofton, the son of a baronet, who had a castle in Ireland. Another daughter Dorothy, married Brigadier Louis Woodhouse, whose family had an estate in Dorset. They had a daughter June who married the Comte de Soissons, from an old French Aristocratic family.

The Indian Civil Service was known as the I.C.S. They were the top men, they ran India, being the administrators, magistrates and judges. It was a very elite service, few in numbers, and very hard to get into. Only those with a first class honours degree from Oxford or Cambridge, stood a chance. Successful applicants took a further year to learn both vernacular and classical language as well as the history of Indian law. A teacher at Oxford took delight in making them count backwards from 100 in Urdu and Punjab, and seeing the shortest time they could do it in.

Before final appointment there was a covenant or contract to be drawn up with the Secretary of State for India; a declaration that they would obey the Viceroy and agree to the condition laid down and regulations of the present government. Corruption was unheard of, they were dedicated men, who went out there to serve the British Empire, as did other such men and women in government service in the colonies.

On arrival in India they became an assistant to a Collector who was an I.C.S. They originally collected revenues. The Collector administrated a 'District', which would cover a vast area, at least the size of England, sometimes twice the size, with a population of at least one million. The number of assistants a collector had, depended on the size of the district, but at most it would be six. After about five years the assistant was eligible to become a collector. The collector was responsible for administrating justice and settling disputes and numerous other duties. Twice a year he would travel to all the outlying villages.

Before the British engineers built roads, railways, bridges, canals, etc. this was done by horseback and sleeping in tents. Even after roads were built many villages were still inaccessible, in which case they had to use a horse.

Sadly the two boys died young young. One of them, Henry Allen Cheshire Gearing, emigrated to Australia, where he married an Australian heiress. At the outbreak of the Great War, he became an officer in the Australian Army, and fought at Gallipoli, which he survived. He was then in France for a while, but had become diabetic, from which he died in England in 1917 aged thirty two. Unfortunately they had no children. His other brother died as a young man in the 1890's, unmarried, which meant the line on that side of the family died out.

It is quite remarkable that some of the descendants of Henry William Gearing, born in Greenwich workhouse in 1822, are listed in Debrett's Peerage! After his wife died, he often used to come back to Greenwich, where he married for a second time, Jane Herdman in 1859, he was still living in Greenwich in 1861. I don't know what became of him after that. My grandfather who was-born in 1858, used to tell us that he had a rich uncle who had lived in India, and owned a string of race horses there, which we found hard to believe. It wasn't until I started to research the family history I found it all to be true, and am now in regular contact with some of his descendants. Sadly grandfather died before I discovered these facts, which he would have loved to have known about.

The younger brother of Henry William, John James Gearing my great grandfather, also went to Greenwich Hospital School. After leaving he was apprenticed to his father as a Lighterman in 1841.

CHAPTER FOUR

GREENWICH 1844 – 1884

In 1844, Henry the tallow chandler died in Greenwich – he was seventy four. He had lived through some great historical events, such as the American War of Independence in 1776, the French Revolution in the 1790's. The Battle of Trafalgar in 1805, and Nelson's 'Lying in State' in the painted hall, in Greenwich Hospital. The abolition of the slave trade in the British Empire in 1807. The Battle of Waterloo in 1815. The first railway locomotive, 'The Rocket', designed by George Stephenson and his son Robert, to run from Stockton to Darlington, in 1825. Also the first crossing of the Atlantic under steam in 1826. The accession to the throne of Queen Victoria in 1837, and the introduction of the penny postage stamp in 1840.

In 1845, his son Henry, now a Lighterman and ex-Navy, went to sea again in the merchant navy, he was 41. I don't know why he left his wife and family, although the children were grown up by then. The two eldest were married. John James, my great grandfather, was twenty and still serving his apprentice ship as a Lighterman, and still living at home as was his younger sister Caroline.

I think Henry was a pretty wild irresponsible character or what is known as 'Jack the Lad'. He had gone to sea at the age of twelve, married when he wasn't in any financial position to,

54

which had caused his son to be born in the workhouse, and now he had deserted his wife, who had to find a job, which she did and became the nurse at 'Trinity Hospital', where she lived-in, although she did not take up the position until the other two children had left home. In the 1851 and 1861, census's he was living in lodgings in Greenwich, he died in one such place in 1862 aged sixty four. My grandfather who was born in 1858, hardly remembered him, but used to tell me that when his grandfather was in the merchant navy, if his ship came up the Thames, he would not wait until it had berthed in London, but swim ashore at Greenwich.

Above: *John James Gearing 1827-1910.*
Below: *His wife Emma nee Sweetlove 1828-1884. My great grandparents.*

John James became a Freeman of the Company of Lightermen in 1845. He was a completely different man to his father, and upheld strong Christian principles all of his life. In 1851, he married Emma Sweetlove, her father had a thriving blacksmith and wheelwright's business in Trafalgar Road, just past the pub called the 'Ship and Billet.' At that time there was

55

Above left: *John Henry Gearing 1858-1948.*
Above right: *His wife, Elizabeth, nee Marchant, 1857-1922.*
My grandparents.

Left: *John Walter Gearing, 1894-1997.*
Above: *His wife, May Emily, nee*
Thompson, 1893-1994.
My parents.

Sweetlove's Cottages and Sweetlove's Yard there. They were an old Kentish family.

John and Emma, moved into a new house at the top end of Pelton Road, which at that time was called Tyler Street North. Next to it was Marsh Lane, which is now Blackwall Lane. From beyond Sweetlove's yard, there was just agricultural land and market gardens, going all the way to Woolwich.

John's younger sister Caroline, married Emma's brother Charles Sweetlove on 15th March 1853, in Greenwich, he was also a blacksmith. On the 10th May 1853 they emigrated to Australia, sailing on 'The Lady Kennaway', which arrived in Melbourne on 15th August 1853, a journey that took three months en-route the ship stopped at Calcutta. I wonder if she had a chance to see her older brother Henry William, who was living there at that time. The ship carried 274 immigrants and merchandise. It was at the time of the Australian gold rush. Charles and Emma, settled in Chewton, a gold digging area near Castlemaine, about 100 miles north of Melbourne. There they raised five daughters, and Charles struck gold, becoming quite a successful miner. Sadly Caroline died in 1869, she was thirty seven. The youngest daughter was only three and the eldest fifteen. Charles was a good man, and very hard working, he built a bungalow which provided them with a comfortable home, and was a well respected citizen in the community. When he died in 1903, an announcement of his death appeared in the local newspaper:

June 10 1903 – Funeral Notice
The friends of the late Mr. Charles J. Sweetlove are respectfully invited to follow his remains to the place of internment, The Chewton Cemetery. The cortege will move from his residence at 3.30pm.

June 11th – Item of News.
The funeral of the late Mr. C. J. Sweetlove of White Horse Gulley, Chewton. Took place yesterday, the remains being fol-

Charles James Sweetlove, 1830-1903.
Castlemaine, Australia.

Grandfather to Australia.
Castlemaine, Australia.

Caroline, daughter of Charles and Caroline Sweetlove, with her three daughters.
Chewton, Australia.

*View of mining area Chewton, 1850's.
Note the cabins and huts they lived in.*

The same view today.

lowed by a large number of people, including the principle residents of Chewton. The children of the Congregational Sunday School marched in front of the hearse and sang a hymn at the grave. The deceased was 72 years of age, and had been a resident of Chewton since 1854. He took a keen interest in the work

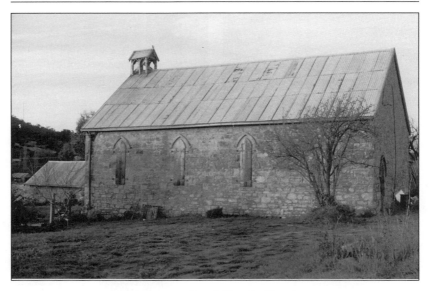

The Congregational Church, Chewton.

of the Congregational Sunday School for many years, and was superintendent.

He lived with his family in White Horse Gully Chewton, which was part of Forest Creek gold diggings – richest alluvial gold area in the world.

John James Gearing and Emma, had nine children, four boys and five girls. Apart from one girl, who died in her-teens, they all lived to a good age. Most of the sons were apprenticed to their father as Lightermen, including my grandfather, John Henry who was born in 1858 in the house in Pelton Road.

1858, was the year of the 'Great Stink' in London, as the Thames was so heavily polluted by sewage, to make matters worse, it was a very hot summer. London was becoming over crowded, and there was no sewage system. The sewers were merely the river's tributaries covered over, and these discharged their stinking contents into the river at low water. As the Thames is a tidal river, when the tide turned, all of it's contents flowed back to London, at the same time more sewage was being emptied into the river. This was mainly due to the invention of the 'Water Closet', as instead of using cesspools as they had in the past, people were flushing their toilets. In fact in 1847, cesspools were made illegal, within a few years some two thousand cesspools were abolished. The affects on the river were appalling, it became an open sewer. In 1800 salmon were swimming up to London, but by the mid-century no fish were to be caught, and the swans could bear the foul water no more.

The smell from the stinking black shore at Westminster, was so overwhelming that the windows of the Houses of Parliament. were hung with sacking impregnated with some strong-smelling disinfectant to make life more tolerable for the members within. Sometimes the House would be compelled to adjourn for the day, on account of the stench. There was even talk of moving to new buildings at Hampton Court. Tons of lime and carbolic were poured into the river without effect, which caused a lot of protest, the following appeared in 'The Oarsmen Guide'!

"The lunging surf of the river steamers stirs from it's oozy bed, in the rear of some friendly obstruction, the sleepy sediment of the tainted Thames. A ceaseless-passage of steam craft ploughs through the sludgy compromise between animal, vegetable and the mineral kingdoms. Feeble rays from the clouded sun glimmer through the murky atmosphere, and play with tarnished glister over the dingy flood. Fishes, wiser in their generation than ourselves, have forsaken in disgust, poisoned by the impurities. The 'Punch' magazine declaimed in 1858.

"Filthy river, filthy river,
foul from London to the Nore,
What art thou but one vast glitter,
One tremendous common shore."

All drinking water came from the Thames, unless one was rich enough to buy it from tanks which were delivered to London. The result was that in the 1830's, 40's and 50's, thousands of people died from cholera and other diseases, which no one connected with the drinking water, I have letter written by my grandfather's cousin, Ann Susan Marshall, aged thirteen, written to her parents in 1849, she attended a private school in Clarence Street, now renamed College Approach, in Greenwich, it reads as follows;

"My dear Parents,
It is with feelings of deepest gratitude that I desire this year to write my annual letter. We cannot forget how many families have lost some relative and how many homes have become entirely desolate by the afflictive visitation of cholera during last autumn. Yet I am permitted by the great mercy of Almighty God, to welcome the return of another Christmas, and to wish you every blessing with the approaching year.

I trust you will find some improvement in my writing, as well as in other branches of my education, since I addressed you, and if it should please God to spare me to mature age, I hope to prove by dutiful conduct how much I feel obliged for the tender care, and means of instruction provided by you.
Your dutiful and affectionate daughter,
Susan.

The situation might have gone on for years, nobody seemed to know what to do about it, finally in 1849 a board of works set up, the head of which was Sir Joseph Bazalgette, 'Comes the day, comes the man', We have to thank him for designing the finest sewage system in the world, which was to save thousands of lives, until then every persons life in the London area, was shortened by twenty years!

Sir Joseph Bazalgette, was born in 1819, and became a very successful engineer, he had worked alongside Brunel, and had designed Hammersmith and Putney Bridges, also many of the great thoroughfares of London, and the construction of the railways. He set to work designing a sewage system for London, but it took him almost ten years of battling with committees and pleading with the government, to put his plan into operation. It wasn't until the members of Parliament were affected themselves, that he was given the go ahead with his plan. An act was passed in sixty days, and within six months work started in 1858, which changed the face of London. Eighty-two miles of sewers on either side of the Thames were constructed going down to the Thames estuary. One thousand one hundred miles of sewers went across the Thames from north to south, connecting outer London. Four pumping stations were built, and a magnificent treatment system was designed. He personally specified every operation, and authorised every plan. It also included a separate water supply.

He also designed the building of the Victoria, Albert and Chelsea Embankments, built between 1864 and 1870, to cover the sewers, at the same time reclaimed thirty seven acres of muddy riverside wasteland.

In the 1860's, my grandfather John Henry was a boy living with his family at the top of Pelton Road, still called Tyler Street North. He used to tell me that opposite their house were corn fields, and they used to take the ripened corn home to their mother, who ground it down for flour. Beyond the corn fields was Greenwich Marsh going down to the river.

In 1867, Marsh Lane (Blackwall Lane) was just a narrow lane, with an odd cottage and farm house. The Pub known as the 'Ship and Billet' was not built until 1869, by which time they were beginning to develop the area. A row of terrace houses had been built on either side of Marsh Lane. the one's on the left, backed on to the corn fields. But behind those on the east or Charlton side more house and roads were being built, as far as Armitage Road, beyond which it was still agriculture. On the opposite side of Woolwich Road, going up the hill, there were more corn fields. farther along where Westcombe Park Police Station is in Combedale Road, was Coombe Farm, which was demolished in 1900, when all the houses and roads on that side of the main road were built.

Higher up the hill, stood Westcombe Manor house, which

Coombe Farm.

had been leased to Mr. Thomas Brocklebank, he was a rich self made man whose fortune was involved in timber and ship building at Deptford. He was the managing director of the General Steam Navigation Company. His lease for the house and the park of 55 acres, was for a term of twenty one years, from Christmas 1827 at £300 per annum. He had formed The General Steam Navigation Company with his brother John, in 1820, for the operation of river steamers on the Thames, which was a very

Coombe Farm.

64

Westcombe Manor.

Woodlands.

Woodlands in the 19th century.

Woodlands in the 1930's when it was a nunnery.

lucrative trade at that time. Their shipyards were at Deptford Creek, from where he launched his river boats.

Thomas Brocklebank and his family lived very well at Westcombe, and he could watch his fleet sailing up and down the Thames. He was also a staunch Tory, and at every election would hold parties at the house. And there would be fairy lights draped from the trees. If the Tory won there would be fireworks, and the hall would be decorated with flags and evergreens.

Brocklebank's next door neighbour was John Angerstein, who was to become the Liberal M.P. but did not interfere with their friendship or business dealings with each other. Brocklebank died in 1843, and his widow went to live at 13, Shooters Hill Road, and the big house was put up for sale.

The following notice appeared in the Greenwich Gazette:

"Mr. Herring, acting for the Executors, to dispose of the remainder of the lease of Westcombe. 55 acres of pasture, park, stabling, farm buildings and offices. Commodious residence approached from a lodge through finely timbered park. It is adapted for the reception of a merchant banker or man of opulence and is presumed to offer peculiar advantages to gentlemen desirous of possessing influence in the Borough of Greenwich with which resident of such property would naturally command."

As the lease had only five years to run, there were no takers, and the Page estate who owned it, would not agree on a new lease, and so the house stood empty until 1855, when it was pulled down. The park became neglected and was used by local people for walks, picnics and other recreational purposes. It remained like that for thirty years, until the 1880's, when plots of land were sold off, and the whole area was developed and is now known as Westcombe Park.

John Henry's father, John James Gearing, had by then become a pilot on the river, and used to bring the big sailing ships from Tilbury to London In about 1871, he apprenticed his son, my grandfather, to him as a Lighterman, following the family tradition and he became a Freeman in about 1888.

In 1884 his mother sadly died aged fifty-six, her husband and family were deeply upset, as they all loved her dearly. She had a stroke which was the third, and was paralysed. In typical Victorian fashion, they all gathered around her bedside, when to their amazement she suddenly sat up, which she hadn't done since the stroke, threw her arms in the air and said "Everything is bright, beautiful and wonderful", she then fell back and died.

CHAPTER FIVE

GREENWICH 1884 – 1914

After his mother died, he joined the merchant navy, and sailed around the world several times. He spent a lot of time in China, travelling all over the country. Whilst there, he used to ship Chinese coolies, across the Pacific to San Francisco to build the railway, from west to east across America. Many of the Chinamen perished on the journey, and were thrown over-board. He also travelled all over Japan, two of the cities he visited were Hiroshima and Nagasaki.

He later sailed to Australia, where he took a job in Sydney, as a waiter. When he had saved some money, he did some more sight seeing and eventually went to Melbourne. From there he went to visit his uncle and cousins at Chewton. Grand-dad stayed with them for four years, helping his uncle, who wanted him to marry one of his daughters, but my grandfather, must have thought the relationship was a bit too close, as they were cousins twice over, as his mother's brother had married his father's sister. In any case, he did not want to settle in Australia, as he did not like the climate, and so he returned to England.

Whilst visiting his best friend Dick West, whose father owned a lot of sailing barges in Greenwich, he met Dick's wife's sister. Her name was Elizabeth Jane Marchant, her father

Thomas John Marchant, 1827-1897.

His wife, Elizabeth, nee Shirley, b.1826.

*Henry William Marchant, b.1867,
their son*

*Elizabeth Jane Marchant, 1857-1922,
their duaghter. My Grandmother.*

Christch Church,
East Greenwich.

Jack with his parents and sister Grace, c1899.

Grandfather's sister, Emma Quick.
1851-1931.

His sister, Caroline May Tomlin.
b.1854.

was a master mariner, and they were of Huguenot stock. She was a nanny/governess to the children of the Secretary of State for India, the Earl of Kimberley.

They were both in their mid-thirties and were married at Christ Church, East Greenwich in 1891. He had by then, started his own business as a shipping chandler at Ballast Quay. He also bought a couple of sailing barges and some houses in Greenwich. As a shipping chandler, he used to supply ships with their supplies.

In 1892, a child Grace was born, followed in 1894 by a son John Walter, who was my father, which completed the family.

Having been away for so long, my grandfather had lost touch with his brothers and sisters, most of whom were married by the time he returned, although, none of his brothers had any children. He was, however, very close to his eldest sister Emma, who had married a man named James Quick, he came from Cornwall, and was a carpenter, he made my grandparents a beautiful mahogany book case as a wedding present. They had married in 1876 and had seven children, the youngest being Frank who was born in 1893, and so was about the same age as my father, and they became very good friends.

Their eldest son Herbert, was born in 1880, and when he was a young man in 1899, the Boer War started, and he joined the City of London Volunteers In 1900 his regiment were sent out to South Africa. Before leaving, he came to see my grandparents, my father was five at the time, but could remember the occasion well. Herbert was playing around with my grandmother, with his revolver, which wasn't loaded, but frightened my father. However, he gave my father sixpence, which was quite a lot in those days. Sadly Herbert died out there in 1901 of enteric fever. His parents were to lose their youngest son Frank also, in the Great War.

Dad was sent to Christ Church School, which he hated, he wanted to mess around on his father's barges and so during the morning break, he would sneak back to his home, where there was a stable with a hay loft above, at the bottom of the garden.

72

Dad used to keep some old clothes up there, which he would change into, and then climb aboard one of his father's barges, and spend the day there. The men were very co-operative, and didn't tell his father. Later he would change back into his school clothes, a Norfolk jacket and starched collar, in time for tea, without his mother being any the wiser. The truancy wasn't discovered until he was eleven, when his parents wanted to send him to 'Boremans', which was part of the Royal Hospital School, and was for sons of men who had not served in the Royal Navy, but had been in the merchant service. They had a better education there and had to pay a small fee and pass an examination which was pretty stiff, naturally dad failed it, which he was to regret for the rest of his life, although it didn't do him much harm.

His mother was a very well-read lady, the bookcase she had been given by her in-laws, was full of all the classics, with which my father was familiar. She loved Shakespeare and Tennyson, and taught him to appreciate them. He learnt many speeches and quotations, which he used to recite at family parties, and could still do so when he was one hundred and two! She also read and spoke fluent French, but was fighting a losing battle as far as dad was concerned, due to the fact that he spent so much time on the river, mixing with some pretty rough characters, and the boys who lived around there. For all that he was an intelligent man, and could converse quite freely with the Queen Mother, and other important people in later years, who all respected him.

In 1908 at the age of fourteen, Jack as he was always called, left school. His parents did not want him to become a Lighterman, so he got a job in a grocer's shop at the Standard, at the top of Westcombe Hill. They used to keep live chickens in the cellar, if a customer wanted to buy one, dad would bring one up for them to inspect. If it was suitable, he would wring it's neck and they would take it away or have it delivered. He also used to do the deliveries by bicycle which he quite enjoyed. But the job wasn't for him, his heart was set on being a Lighterman. So he went to see his grandfather, who persuaded his father to apprentice him.

His grandfather sadly died in 1910 aged eighty four. He was living in Trinity Hospital, where he had moved, when he retired in the 1890's. His mother had been the nurse there in the 1860's. Dad was seventeen and remembers him quite well, he said he was a very kind gentle man, a good husband and father, but quite strict with his sons. He did not use bad language and would not allow his sons to do so either, and would not allow cards in the house.

He was a devout Christian, when he was dying all his family including his sons, gathered around his bed singing hymns he doesn't appear to have been like his father. I like to think he was more like his grandfather, the tallow chandler from Sussex, who I have a feeling was a good honest man, as were my father and grandfather.

In 1910, dad was apprenticed to the water, aged sixteen, and started work on one of his father's sailing barges called 'The

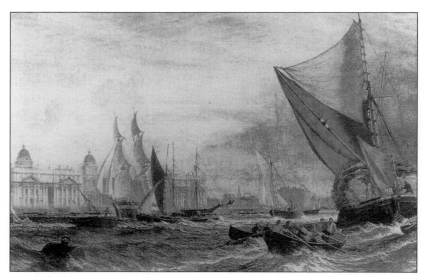

Thames sailing barge, laden with hay.

Star'. There was just a skipper and himself. One of their main jobs, was to load the barge with horse dung which they would pick up from collecting points by the river in London and take it down to Faversham in Kent, where farmers were waiting with hay to take back to feed the horses. The farmers would then load their carts with the manure, which was used to fertilize the land. There was also a brick works there and they would sometimes return with a load of bricks as there was a lot of building going on in London at that time. The barges on the north side of the river always went to Essex, and it was an unwritten law that they never crossed over.

There was always a crew of just two, on the sailing barges, the skipper and a mate or an apprentice. They each had their own small cabin, lined with mahogany wood, and there was a small galley with a stove in it, at the back of the barge or 'aft' as it was called. In the 'foc'sle', they kept all the ropes and sails etc.

Jack's skipper was Tommy Price, who taught dad a lot, and they got on very well. He would always give Jack a third of what he earned on each trip, which could sometimes take two three days.

On one occasion, they were tied up at Faversham, as Tommy the skipper lived at Ramsgate, which was quite near. He told Jack he was going home for the night, and left dad in charge, and told him to clean up the barge – scrubbing the decks etc. There he met a 'down-and-out' who he took pity on, and so invited him on to the barge where he gave him a good meal. As he hadn't got anywhere to sleep for the night, he let him sleep in the skipper's bunk. The next morning when dad got up, the man had gone.

When the skipper returned, they immediately set sail, when they got out into the middle of the Thames, Tommy went down to change into his working clothes. A short time later he shouted up to Jack, "Where are my clothes?". The down-and-out had obviously taken them, so Tommy wasn't too happy. But he soon got over it, and they took the barge to Woolwich, where Tommy took Jack, to see the famous boxer of the time, Jack

Johnson fighting at East Ham Palace.

About a year later, he felt he had learnt all there was to know about sailing barges, and got a job with the London Lighterage Department. Whilst working for them, he fell overboard, his father had always told him, if that happened to shout out, which he did, but nobody heard him, and he drifted down to Woolwich, by which time he was exhausted, fortunately somebody heard him and threw him a line, and he was picked up by a tug.

In 1912, Jack was crossing Blackheath with some friends, it was a Sunday and he was wearing his best suit. Some young ladies passed, and one of them caught Jack's eye. It was a hot day, and she had a parasol, when a gust of wind caught it and blew it inside out. Jack offered to get it repaired in order to meet her again. Her name was Mabel Emily Thompson, but always known as May, and so began a romance which was to last for over eighty years. She was a year older than him, having been born in 1893. She also came from a Lighterage family, going back to the middle of the 18th century in Bermondsey. She had lost her parents at an early age, and went to live with her older sister, whose husband was a compositor in a printing firm.

May did very well at school, and was always top of her class, she won a lot of prizes. At thirteen she was top of the school, they decided they could not teach her anymore, so she taught the younger pupils. She left school at fourteen, and her sister made her get a job in a clothes factory. May hated it, and found a job in a book printing firm in the City. There she trained as a book binder, which was a skilled occupation, she became very good at it, and enjoyed her work. By then, she and Jack were courting but everything was to change, two years later in 1914, when the Great war was declared.

CHAPTER SIX

THE GREAT WAR 1914 – 1922

Jack immediately volunteered for the Royal Navy. May was hoping to get married but Jack didn't think it was a good idea, in case he got killed and he did not want her to become a young widow.

May also wanted to do her bit to help the war effort, so she got a job at Woolwich Arsenal, making munitions where she was in the danger building which was surrounded by water because of the risk of explosions.

In the meantime, Jack was sent to a naval training depot at Crystal Palace, where they had to do route marches across Epsom Downs. Whilst there he volunteered for the balloon section, and had to go up in a basket to spot Zeppelins, getting up to 500 feet, if he saw or heard one, he had to call down.

Jack in his sailors uniform.

Women making munitions at Woolwich Arsenal.

The basket under the balloon had a rope attached to it and was secured to something on the ground. If the rope snapped, he had a grappling hook which he would lower down until it snagged on something.

He was later posted to Chatham, and then on to Devonport, where in 1915 he joined the 'Theseus', a cruiser. He hadn't been on her long before they set sail for the Mediterranean, and then on to Gallipoli.

They arrived in Mudros and took on board a battalion of the East Yorks regiment, to fight what was to become one of the hardest battles ever fought. The regiment consisted of four hundred men, mostly new recruits, fresh from training, few had seen action. Every sailor was given two soldiers to look after. They gave them their hammocks, and made sure they ate well, and even gave them their rum ration, as they knew they were going to hell on earth.

As they approached Suvla Bay on the night of 6th August, it

was darkness before the dawn. Jack stood by the gangway which had been fitted over the stern to allow the troops to walk down into motor lighters. As the soldiers followed each other down with their rifles, one got hit by a sniper, and screamed out. Jack told him to shut up and put up with the pain or he would frighten the others – that was his first scream of war, and he was frightened himself. He took him down to the sick bay.

He was then put on a raft with a 5-inch gun and towed by a pinnace into shore to land with the troops. He stayed with them for a day and then a picket boat came and took him back on board.

Throughout the time they were there they bombarded the Turks' positions, with their guns. He had never had any experience in firing a gun, but was made a breach loader, on one of the 6-inch. guns. During this time they were fired on constantly by the Turks, who were up in the hills.

On one occasion the anchor failed, it meant the ship was in trouble, so Jack had to help the diver with his equipment. As they worked down below the diver talked to him on a rope. The Turks must have spotted what they were doing, and all the time they were shooting at him. But he had to stay by the rope and work out what the diver wanted. When he had finished his work, he tugged at the rope and he got him up, and still the Turks continued firing at them.

Each day when there was a lull, they would go ashore and collect the wounded, some were in a very bad way, and Jack said they were all so young.

Each Sunday they would have a Church Service aboard the ship, and the crew would sing the hymns as loudly as they could to inspire the soldiers their favourites were 'Onward Christian Soldiers' and 'Fight The Good Fight'. On other days, when scrubbing the decks, they sang more hymns and songs, anything that was rousing to cheer the soldiers up, and to let them know they were not alone.

When Jack went ashore, he saw a lot of Turkish prisoners. They were all badly dressed and always wanted boots, they were so poor, but were wonderful fighting men, they wouldn't give up – we could see them from the ship.

Everybody was getting very depressed towards the end, as we weren't succeeding at all, and losing a lot of men and ships. Every day, they were bringing in different men, different faces, all were tired and beaten.

It was summer and very hot, with flies getting into everything, it was unbearable and made matters worse for the soldiers ashore.

Then as autumn came, and things were getting worse on the land, even with reinforcements. It was a picture of failure, being fought out by very brave men, but in spite of everything, they kept fighting on.

In the end the allied forces, made up from Australia, New Zealand, and Britain decided to withdraw, and so on 20th December 1915, after eight months, the evacuation took place on a very dark night by barges loaded with men horses and guns, to the waiting ships, and never lost a man, everybody kept absolutely quiet so as not to arouse the Turks.

Jack's ship the 'Theseus', then spent almost a year at Mudros, patrolling the area. Early in 1917, the ship sailed to Crete, and anchored at Suda Bay. Whilst they were there, they took over a mental hospital, and the ships two surgeons, in their red aprons, were in charge. A number of ship were torpedoed-in the area, and the crew from the 'Theseus', would go out in their pinnaces to pick up survivors. The first lot they picked up, were from a troop ship. The wheelwrights made handles, and canvas was sewn on to them to make stretchers. They raced out as fast as they could to pick up all the survivors. When they towed them in they had to make sure, they didn't bump the wharf. They then carried them on the stretchers up to the hospital.

On one occasion, Jack gave a piggy-back to one of the wounded. He was a cockney and had his leg hanging off. About half way to the hospital he said "Give us a fag Jack", so dad rolled him one, and they both had a smoke, he then got him to the hospital. When Jack went to see him the next morning, he had died. He had lost too much blood.

A few days later, another troopship packed with men was hit. The U-boat fired another torpedo, and a Japanese destroyer, (they were on our side in that war), which was accompanying the troopship, deliberately turned itself into the path of the torpedo, and was badly damaged, but made it back to the harbour. Jack's crew helped their dead and wounded ashore. The Japanese then cremated their dead. The shipwrights on the 'Theseus' made a lot of wooden boxes, to take the remains of the dead, back to Japan. Jack thought it was a very brave thing the Captain of the Japanese ship had done. The 'Theseus' then sailed to Malta for repairs, where it stayed for a few months.

Whilst Jack was in the Navy, he wrote regularly to his parents, mainly addressed to his mother, who he loved dearly, and always wanted to please her. She kept some of his letters, which I have, and here are extracts from them:

This one was written in 1914, when he first joined the Navy, and was stationed at Crystal Palace, in the Benbow Battalion;

"Dear Mother and Father,
I got back alright, I am very pleased to say, I thank you for your kindness towards Mabel, you must not think I have forgotten you Mother, because I like that girl. I always remember my good kind parents, and love them, but mother you must remember you were an orphan once and you always taught me to be kind, so I have only got your ways. I know the worry you have had with poor Grace (his sister), but it was a God send to my idea, and you will have a change of luck soon. You must still laugh like you use to and dance and sing.

I did not go on the draft today as I thought, a lot did, but I don't want to be in a hurry, it does make me look a liar when I tell people I am going and say goodbye, so I will say no more.

Mabel did have a bad cold, but she is a good Christian girl, she puts me in mind of you.

Well dear, The King came unexpectantly today and inspected us. He does look worried and not at all well, I was right close to him with-

in a few yards, so I saw him well. He looks quite ten years older, I would not like to have his job.

Well dear Mother, I will close now hoping you and dad are quite well. I am fine, thanks to the Lord, and hope you will get over your trouble, so cheer up and do pray for me, as I need it so.

From your only and ever loving son, Jack.

P.S. Please correct my spelling if you can find wrong words."

This one was written in March 1915 from Scotland:

"Dear Mother and Father,

I hope you enjoyed your little gift, I wish I could do more as I know you deserve it. Well I hope you receive this parcel and dad puts on the smoking hat, and has a jolly good smoke, and get that serge made up into a nice costume.

Well I don't suppose the letters will reach me for a while, do not worry if you do not hear from me for a week or so. I will be away for a time and as soon as I get ashore, I will let you know how I am getting on and will send you some presents from Scotland. It will be no use of you answering my letter before you receive another one after this.

Well dear folks, I have some work to do and I must bring my letter to a close, trusting to God you are quite well.

From Your loving boy Jack,

Pray for me mother. Xxxxx"

This one is from Chatham, just before he sailed to Gallipoli:

"Dear Mother,

I received your letter and postal order of 5/- and thank you very much. I am pleased you told me off, it was a very bad letter, please forgive me and teach me still, I've got a lot to learn. I hope to be go away about Friday. Well mother I have tried to correct myself, I hope this one is satisfactory, but I only have a few minutes to spare. The boys often ask to see your photo when my box is open, and I ask them your age and they say 45-50 so you must look young, and I let them think it. (She would have been fifty eight). In your next letter let me know about Grace. (His sister). Well mother I think I will close as there is not much news I can tell you, give my love to dad.

From your loving and obedient son,

Jack XXXXXX"

I don't know the date of the following letter, but it was when he was at sea:

"My dear kind mother,
Very many thanks for your kind and welcome letter which I received this morning dated Nov 8th. It's the first for a long while, so you know how long it takes to reach me. I hope mine is not long in reaching you. I am going on fine and keeping in the best of health, although I would like to get ashore, it is nearly six months since I was ashore. The same old things every day I cannot understand why, and there is plenty of work to do so it makes it very monotonous, that's the only trouble I got, so I must get used to it. I don't suppose I will be with you at Xmas, but very likely soon after, and then I will make it so happy, so don't worry, everything I will make up for, a little more the same as when I left likely. I have not done my best in helping you and dad, but if I get another chance I will try to do better and be a little more cheerful. It does one good be away it helps one to learn their faults and improve.
Well my brave mother I don't mind being away so long as I know your not worrying over me, although we don't have it all honey, the fighting part is not the trouble at all, it is the very hard work and no play, you know when I say that it must be true. I have not been ashore yet and expect I will fall over when I do, days in, days out rolling about without seeing any life, what a life, but never mind, it is all for my home and children, not mine, other peoples, anybody would think I was an old married man, to read my letters. Well we had some very cold weather and snow and we have been wet with the rough weather, and you feel it after the hot weather The decks froze over when the water was there and so you can guess how cold it is over here. Well that's all the trouble I got so I think I can battle through that, don't you.

I was eating some biscuits and I broke one of my teeth, I will wait until I go to AWD then get it repaired. I am informed in your last letter that Mr. Bailey was going to throw you out of home, the pig, I know what a bluffer he is, tell dad to watch him, I know you had a lot of trouble with him. (His father was in dispute with Mr. Bailey over some property he owned, of which Mr. Bailey was the ground landlord. It eventually went to court, and unfortunately grandfather lost the case, which bankrupted him).

Well I must bring this Xmas letter to a close, you must excuse my spelling and writing, as I am dead beat and longing to get into my hammock I hope you and dear old father are in the best of health, and will have a happy Xmas.

From your loving son, Jack. XXXXXXX"

This one is dated 9th Feb. 1917:

"My darling Mother and Father,
I was so pleased to receive your loving letter of the 14th.Jan I often wonder how you are going after all this time, how I miss you, I can tell you are a good true and straight forward and a splendid scholar, those Shakespeare sayings, how they come to me. I know if I come home, that book case will be used by me. You used to say to me, I would take after you, I think I will. I have read that book the "Haven", you sent to me it was very nice indeed.

I am pleased to hear you make Mabel happy, she is a good girl. I am glad you like her, it is very good of her to give you a present. I hope she still comes to see you. Let me know how things fair with her, I have not heard from her this mail. I am very pleased to hear Grace is getting better that stops me thinking a lot. Well dear, I have answered all you asked me. How is dad going on? I have great hope of being home sometime this year. I often look at your photo, you seem prettier each time I look. Oh well, lets hurry up and meet you, I believe I will eat you all up when I do, so cheerio I am still in the pink.

From your loving son, Jack. XXXXXXXX"

N.B. He had not had any leave for three years.

6th July 1918, Naples.

"My dear Mother,

I have received your letter. I am pleased to say I am still keeping well, though the change of climate has upset my system. I have been in hospital and just come out feeling weak. I have a rash over my face, the matron said I had a slight fever, it could not be much, because I was jolly soon out, I am pleased I was, for they starved me, after having chicken soup and a dozen other nice dishes which we get on the ship, though I am making up for it now, putting plenty of good grub down my belly.

Well dear your letters are short and very nice and the writing very good, I wish I could write like you, it shows character. I often think now how you spoke when I was a small boy and I did not take any interest. I can see now you are very clever, How I would like to take you around these places, we are lying quite close to Mount Vesuvius, a volcano, which does look beautiful at night with the deep blue sky and the sun setting at the back and the sea glittering below. In the day I go in the City and see the Roman buildings and statues. If I had the money I should like to go to Rome which is only seven hours from here. I shall be sorry if I lost the opportunity. But I am here for a month or more so I might get a chance. And then there is Pompeii, where the earth-wake was, that's all debris.

Well mother the war has done me a lot of good. When I leave here we go to Alexandria and then to Bombay India, and then to the States, so I don't know when I shall come home, unless I have the luck to get another ship before this one sails. But that's her route and it's no good expecting me home for at least another year

Well mother, I hope and trust you are both well, and dad's still at work. I was sorry to hear about Grace, I know she is a very hard case, and you and dad has a trying time with her, but in any condition keep her there until the war is over, or you will be sorry. Well mother we must still carry on through lifes trials and be satisfied as we are, and so life goes on. There is trouble where ever we look, and I could tell you some which you would never believe, though I seldom do.

Well mother I will close now and get into my bunk with the flies and mosquitos, and think and dream of home.

From your loving son, Jack. XXXXXX"

10th August 1918.

"My Darling Mother & Dad,
I am writing your weekly letter, I always try to write at least once a
week. There will be times when I will not be able to write, as I shall be
on my way to Calcutta, which will be six or seven weeks trip and you
cannot post letters at sea.
Well mum everything is merry and bright with me. I have got over
the grand fever, but still got a rash, but that will wear off as I get accli-
matized. I have been ashore here at Naples, which I told you is very
pretty, though the place is very poor and full of beggars. All the
Roman Catholic countries seem the same, I put it down to the reli-
gion. There are plenty of places I shall visit while I am here, which will
be six or seven weeks yet. I shall let you know if I get a chance when
I am leaving so you will expect any letters before I get to the next port,
which will out East. I am pleased I am going to India, what a chance
of seeing the world this war has brought for some. I think I have
gained twenty years experience more than I should. Of course moth-
er, I feel home sick now that I am a married man, I never used to
before. But how sweet it will be when I come home to find you nurs-
ing your grandson. That's trusting the wife pulls through all right,
she is strong so she ought. You will have to give her your "wack" of
milk. And how is old dad going on? is he still working?, trust he is
not sick and also you mother. You are both getting on in years now,
how is your home going along, I do like the place in which you live. I
wish Mabel would live there it would be better for her health, any-
where that is near you. I wish I was on Blackheath now in England
and it's rain How I miss it, and green Greenwich Park. The weather
here is very hot and a lot of English men have been down with fever,
I cannot make it out. I have done three years in these conditions.
Thank God I am well now, praying you are both the same.
From your most loving and affectionate son Jack."
N.B. Mabel was still living with her sister in East Ham, where
her husband worked. Mabel gave birth to a daughter in
December 1918, named Eve.

In 1916, Jack's cousin, who was also his best friend, was killed at the battle of the Somme in France, he was twenty one. The whole family were devastated, as he was such a likable lad, with a very happy disposition. Sadly, his mother had lost her eldest son Herbert during the Boer War, and now she had lost her youngest Frank, in the Great War. The inscription on his grave in one of the War Grave Cemeteries, reads as follows:

In Memory of
Frank James Quick
Acting Bombardier
L/6396
'A' Bty., 167th Bde., Royal Field Artillery
who died on
Sunday, 30th July 1916. Age 21.

Additional Information: Son of Mr. and Mrs. E. Quick, of 26, Wearside Rd., Lewisham, London.

Commemorative Information

Cemetery: CATERPILLAR VALLEY CEMETERY, LONGUE-VAL, Somme, France Grave Reference/ XIV. A. 32.

In October 1917, Jack's ship was in Malta for repairs and a re-fit, and he was due for some leave, the first for three years. He wrote to Mabel telling her to put up the banns, at Christ Church, E. Greenwich, for the 17th November. He also told her not to have a wedding dress made, as he would be bringing some Maltese silk home for the purpose. And so they were married on the appointed day, with May wearing her lovely dress, which we still have in the family, and is now used as a Christening gown, for her descendants. This marriage was to last for seventy-seven years, which I will write about later.

They spent their honeymoon in Chatham, where Jack joined another ship, which was to sail to the Far East and India. May

Jack and May's wedding, Christ Church, 17th November 1917.

continued to work at the Royal Arsenal, still living with her sister in East Ham.

In 1919, Jack was discharged from the Royal Navy, after spending some time in Canada and Ireland.

May was expecting another baby, and she was not getting on with her sister, and the house was too crowded. Jack had to find another place to live pretty quickly, which he did, in East London.

Jack soon got a job with the Lighterage Department of the South East Metropolitan Gas Co. which in those days was a co-partnership. At that time they were only taking on ex-servicemen. It was a very good firm to work for, as they were all co-partners. It had a wonderful community and family ethos about it.

It was situated at the bottom of Blackwall Lane, where the Meridian Dome is now situated. There were sports fields and allotments for the men going right up to Horn Lane behind Tunnel Avenue. There was also a big concert hall, which was called the 'Livesey Institute', named after Dr. Livesey, who had been the founder of the company. We had wonderful children's parties there, and sports days, dad also had an allotment which came in very useful.

CHAPTER SEVEN

CHILDHOOD MEMORIES 1922 – 1939

In 1922, Jack's mother sadly died of cancer, she was sixty five. It affected him very deeply, as she had always had such a profound influence on him, and he loved and respected her dearly. I don't think he ever really got over her loss. She had died on Whit-Sunday, and for the rest of his long life, he took flowers to church on the anniversary of her death.

She was a devout Christian, and taught him the catechism at an early age. She took him and his sister Grace, to Christ Church every Sunday. Jack continued to attend Church every Sunday, for the rest of his life, he was still taking holy communion, well past his 102nd. Birthday.

He had inherited his strong faith, from both sides of his family. His mother's ancestors were Huguenots, they were French Protestants, and had been persecuted through the ages in France, which was predominantly a Roman Catholic country. On the 24th August 1572, thousands of Protestant men, women and children, were dragged from their homes in Paris, and butchered. It was known as the St. Bartholomew day massacre. From then on thousands were driven into exile, over the next 200 years. Many settled in the London area of Spitalfields, mainly working as silk weavers. Jack's mother was born there in 1857.

I have already written about the Gearing's being non-conformists, at the time of Queen Elizabeth I. They were also persecuted for their faith. Although, when Henry Gearing moved from Sussex to Greenwich in 1795, there is no evidence that he continued to follow the Baptist religion, he probably found it too repressive in Sussex, which may have been one of the reasons for moving away.

As children, we all attended Sunday school regularly, and my brother and I were confirmed at school.

In 1923, Jack's sister Grace sadly died. She had been ill for some time, and was thirty-one years old, and had never married.

By 1923, Jack and May had three children. Eve was born in 1918, Carole in 1920 and John in 1922, but they were not happy living in East London. Eventually Jack's father found a house for sale in Halstow Road, East Greenwich where they moved, and I was born there in 1924. Iris was born in 1927, which completed the family. The house in Halstow Road, was a typical outer London terrace house with bay windows, it had a sitting room, dining room and a large kitchen and scullery at the back, with three double bedrooms and bathroom upstairs. There was a small garden which backed onto a private cemetery, which belonged to Greenwich Hospital, where the pensioners had been buried, and was now used for the burial of the staff and pupils of the Royal Hospital School. There was a high wall separating our garden from it. It was always well maintained, and not open to the public as it is now. There were plenty of trees there and the only noise we heard was bird song.

Halstow Road was quite well situated, as it has a school where we were all sent as infants. Also it is close to Westcombe Park railway station, where there was a post office and some nice shops, including Barker's, a high class grocer's and wine merchants, and it is only about a ten minute walk to Blackheath and Greenwich Park.

Jack and May were wonderful parents. They led good lives, and set us a fine example, they drank and smoked very little. Every penny my father earned, went into the home, which he was always improving, he was the original DIY man. He had a

The author aged one year in 1925.

20, Halstow Road, East Greenwich, 1926. L to R: dad, grandfather, and mother. In front L to R: Eve, Carole, Albert and John on the tricycle.

With Iris on the beach at Cliftonville, 1929.

With brother John, 1934.

great friend, who he had known since childhood, Steve Fletcher, who was a builder and owned a lot of property in Greenwich.

They set about modernising the house, by bringing it up to 1920 standards! They built a conservatory at the back, which housed the big old mangle, coal bunker, place to hang washing, playroom, and above all, it meant we did not have to go outside to the lavatory, which was a great blessing.

He also removed the copper from the scullery, and replaced it with a gas cooker, so that the old scullery, now became the kitchen and the old kitchen became the living room. They also put a geyser in the bathroom, and knocked down the wall separating the dining and sitting room, which made a nice big room for the many parties we had.

Mother loved children, all our friends called her 'Aunty May'. Every so often she would make a batch of toffee apples to give to the children, we were lucky to have any left for ourselves.

She was a wonderful mother, but certainly didn't spoil us in any way. During the school holidays she would arrange lots of treats for us. She loved taking us to London, especially Hyde Park, which we knew as well as Greenwich Park. We usually went by bus or tram to Parliament Square, and then across Horse Guards Parade into St. James's Park and then through Green Park and onto Hyde Park, where we would spend the day by Serpentine and listen to the band. On other occasions, we would walk up Whitehall to Trafalgar Square, up Regent Street to Piccadilly Circus and then along Oxford Street, where she loved to look at all the shops, and then on to Hyde Park. There was nothing we did not know about London.

We never missed a Royal event, mother would get us all up early, and catch a train. I remember in 1935, watching King George V and Queen Mary, drive up the Mall during the Silver Jubilee celebrations. We also saw his funeral procession, the following year. Mother got us up at about 5am. It was a cold wet January morning, and still dark whilst we waited at Westcombe Park station. When we got to London, there were thousands of people already there, and we found a place on Horse Guards

Parade. It was a very sombre occasion, I remember seeing the old Prince of Wales and his three brothers following the gun carriage on foot.

We also stood outside Buckingham Palace when the Duke of Kent married Princess Marina and the Duke of Gloucester married Alice, Lady Montague Douglas Scott. Quite often when we were in Hyde Park, we would pass by the garden of 145, Piccadilly where the Duke and Duchess of York lived, with their daughters Elizabeth and Margaret, hoping we might get a glimpse of the Princesses playing in the garden. A few years later, after their father had become King, and they were living in Buckingham Palace, mother read in the paper that their house in Piccadilly was open to the public, so she took us there. We were shown the main rooms downstairs, and then taken to the top of the huge house, to the nursery. There was a wide landing with a gate at the top of the stairs, and we were told the Princesses used to cycle around the landing. Sadly the house was bombed during the Blitz.

We never missed the Lord Mayor's Show, which was quite a spectacular event in those days, one year there were elephants taking part in it, and I seem to remember that a woman in the crowd had her foot trodden on by one, which must have been a very painful experience.

Mother also took us to see the pantomime at the Lyceum Theatre every year. Dad who was much more serious, and loved Shakespeare, used to take the older children to the 'Old Vic' theatre where they saw Macbeth one year, when the famous actor, Charles Laughton, was playing the main part.

When we were very young mother would take us to Greenwich Park to feed the ducks on the lake, but when we were old enough to go alone, we spent Saturdays and school holidays either on Blackheath or Greenwich Park. Mother would pack us sandwiches and a bottle of Tizer, and off we would go for the day. It was quite safe in those days, as there was very little traffic on the quiet roads leading to the Heath, and we had never heard of children being molested.

Blackheath was a marvellous place, all undulating with huge dips full of gorse bushes, which had been sand pits. It was ideal to play 'Cowboys and Indians', and for tobogganing when it snowed. We also spent a lot of time in the Park, quite often with our bikes, as there were a lot of paths and the broad avenue leading up to the observatory.

We often used to go along Shooters Hill Road, to Castle and Jack Woods, which was quite an adventure. Before the houses in Wricklemarsh Road and the other houses around there were built in the 1930's, it was all farm land, with cows grazing. Opposite the pub 'The Dover Patrol', which hadn't been built then, was a dairy farm, where we used to watch the cows being milked. All the way along Rochester Way, up to Well Hall Road, were orchards. Sometimes we would go down Pond Road and Foxes Dale, which were unmade roads then, at the bottom was a little wooden bridge which crossed a stream called the 'Quaggy', which flowed through to Lewisham. Beyond the stream were meadows going all the way to Kidbrooke Station.

Kidbrooke Farm.

95

During the war there was an R.A.F. Camp there.

To get to Blackheath and Greenwich Park, we had to go along Coleraine Road. Halfway along on right or west side of the road, was a gap between the houses, which took us down a bank, to a place we called the 'Combe'.

At the bottom of the bank, there was a dirty old pond, and some old water tanks and boilers, which had been dumped there. It was in a big field with bushes, which was a wonderful place to explore and play, especially for boys. The field was enclosed by the houses in Coleraine Road, Westcombe Park Road, Foyle Road and Humber Road. It was all that was left of the garden of Westcombe Manor which stood where Peacham Road is, off Humber Road. It had been a beautiful garden at one time, with ornamental ponds. When the old house was pulled down and the fifty-five acre park surrounding it was built on during the 1880's, for some unknown reason, that was left.

We later moved to 21, Humber road, which is opposite Peacham Road, and wasn't built until after the war, before that there were houses there which were bombed during the Blitz. The gap in Coleraine Road which led down to the 'Combe', is now occupied by Belfast Park. I have never been there, since these roads were built, so I do not know what it is like now.

21, Humber Road, house on the right. From the back of the house we had a magnificent view of the Thames, from Tower Bridge to Woolwich.

At the bottom of Mycenae Road, where it joins Beaconsfield Road and Humber Road, there was another small field where we used to play. I have read from the books of 'Neil Rhind', who has done an extensive study of Blackheath, that when the surrounding area was developed, the field was meant to have a hotel built on it. But the new residents, did not want a licenced premises near them, and petitioned the licensing justices to refuse to grant a licence, and so the hotel was not built. In the late 1930's about six houses were built on the site.

At the top of Beaconsfield Road where it joins Hardy Road, there is a municipal garden dividing the two roads, before the war, there were tennis courts there, the space had originally been kept to build a church, but when the area was developed in the 1880's, the builders ran out of money. On Sunday afternoons, after Sunday School, we often used to watch the tennis.

On the Beaconsfield Road side, where there are now flats, there were three large detached houses. Gilnockie, Kingsbridge and Fairfax House, which was the biggest, and was directly opposite the tennis courts. It was a rambling Tudor style house and stood back from the road, with a semi circular driveway. It also had a huge garden, which stretched right down to Mycenae Road, and butted on to the garden of Woodlands House, which was then a nunnery. There was a large lake at the bottom of the garden, with a boat house.

Fairfax was owned by Mr. Dence, who was a director of Messrs. Johnson & Phillips, an electrical engineering and cable making firm in Charlton.

He had been the Mayor of Greenwich in 1922-1923, and an LCC councillor from 1919 to 1934, and chairman in 1933.

Quite often when we were sitting on the seat watching the tennis, he would come over to us and invite us into his garden, and allow us to take a boat out on the lake. He was also an amateur astronomer, and had his own small observatory in the garden, which he would take us into and look through his giant telescope, and tell us about the stars and planets. He was one of the kindest men I have ever known. He also allowed the garden to be used for garden parties and theatricals. Sadly he died in the 1930's, and the house was sold to the Courtauld family.

At the outbreak of the war, the house was requisitioned by the R.A.F. as the headquarters of the balloon section who manned the barrage balloons on Blackheath, mainly by girls or W.A.A.Fs as they were called. The girls also slept in the house.

One of my sister's, Carole, was a W.A.A.F. which stood for Womens Auxiliary Air Force. Carole was stationed somewhere in England, and as our mother was ill, managed to get a compassionate posting to Kidbrooke but slept at Fairfax House. As we only lived in the next road, she would often sleep at home, which was against rules and regulations. One night, we had a terrible air raid, when Carole returned to the house the following morning, it had received a direct hit, and most of the girls were killed. Also during the war, the tennis courts were turned into allotments. After the war the other two houses were demolished, and the present flats built on the site.

We were very lucky to have been brought up in Blackheath and Greenwich, as we had such a variety of places to go to, without our mothers having to worry about us.

Another of our favourite activities, was to ride on the Woolwich Free Ferry which were old paddle steamers. We used to love to stand on a gallery overlooking the engine room and watch the huge highly polished pistons, going backwards and forwards, to drive the paddles.

In the summer mother would always take us for a trip down the river on one of the paddle steamers, which ran from Tower Bridge, calling at Greenwich, Southend, Margate and Ramsgate. They were called 'The Golden Eagle' and 'Crested Eagle'. I believe it cost about 2/6d. for adults, and 1/6d. for children. We would spend the day at one of those places, and catch the boat back at about 5pm. As there was a bar on board, or maybe some of the male passengers, brought some booze aboard, it always turned out to be a merry evening. Both these boats were used to evacuate the troops from Dunkirk, where they were badly damaged, and not used after the war.

On Sunday mornings, we usually went over the college where we would watch the boys from the Royal Hospital School parade in front of the Queen's House. When the parade was over, the school band would strike up, and the boys would march across Nelson Road to the Chapel in the Naval College. They would be led by a little drum major, who would swing his

Thames paddle steamer

baton over the wrought iron gates, and catch it on the other side. There were always crowds of people there, and all the traffic would be held up.

We would then go on to St. Alphege's Church, where we would meet our grandfather after the service, and then accompany him back to his flat in Trinity Hospital, going round by the river along Crane Street and Highbridge, which used to be a hive of activity, with men repairing their boats, and the Greenwich Rowing Club attending to theirs. It always smelt of tar and ropes along there. Grandad would then come to us for the lunch and stay for the rest of the day.

We were all very fond of our grandfather, he was a very kind gentle man. We used to love to visit him in Trinity Hospital. He had moved there after his wife died in the 1920's.

Trinity Hospital, was built in 1613, by Henry Howard, the Earl of Northampton, for old Greenwich gentlemen. It was also known as Norfolk College, as Henry Howard also founded

The courtyard, Trinity Hospital.

The chapel, Trinity Hospital.

The garden, Trinity Hospital.

another Trinity Hospital, in the village of Castle Rising, in Norfolk, for elderly ladies, and the two are connected. During the last war, as the hospital was so close to the river, which got the worst of the bombing, the men were evacuated to the home in Norfolk, including my grandfather, who wasn't at all happy there, and so my mother brought him back to live with us, where he stayed until he died at the age of ninety.

In my grand-father's time, we entered through the main front door which was always open during the day.

On entering, you go through an arch, and are confronted with a beautiful courtyard, with a fountain in the middle of a lily pond. The courtyard is surrounded by a cloister, with square pillars, each one connected to the next by a gothic style arch, and has a paved stone floor.

If you turn left, after passing a couple of doors, you turn right to proceed up the left hand side of the courtyard and pass a couple of the mens apartments, you then come to a door, which is the entrance to the chapel. In the chapel there was a figure of the founder, kneeling in prayer, on a plinth.

Continue on, and you pass two more apartments, before turning right, and pass two more. You then come to an arched doorway, opposite the main entrance. This doorway, leads to the garden door. On the right is a beautiful wide Jacobean staircase.

The garden is about an acre in size, and surrounded by a high wall. It is mainly laid to lawns, with shrubs and flower beds. There used to be one or two lovely old mulberry trees, which I think were as old as the building. They used to bear a lot of fruit, which we were able to pick and take home to mother who would make jam. We also used to be invited to garden parties, which were held there.

Coming back to the cloister again, turn left and pass two more apartments, and then turn right. On the left was a door leading to what my grandfather called the sub-hall, I believe it had been the men's dining hall, before they had their own kitchens. It was and still is a communal sitting room.

In grandad's time, there was a big open fire, with a high

backed settle either side, and a rack on the wall, containing long white clay pipes.

Continuing along the cloister, there was a stable door, which was the butler's pantry, where the butler would spend all day doing his chores, from there he could see everyone who came in, and would tick us off, if he caught us running or mis-behaving. Next to the pantry was the Warden's kitchen, who had a suite of rooms upstairs, over the front of the building.

After passing the pantry, you turned right, passing the door to the nurse's flat. My grandfather's, grandmother had been the nurse there in the 1850's and 60's. Also his father had been a resident there, after losing his wife, from the 1890's until he died in 1910, so we have a very long association with the Home.

Upstairs, where my grandfather had his rooms, was similar to down below. If you turned right and then left, halfway down was a bathroom and toilets. Halfway up on the opposite side was the committee room, which was beautifully panelled in oak, and is where the trustees from the Mercer's Company in London, come every so often to hold meetings with the warden.

My grandfather aged 70 in 1928.

Upstairs, always seemed cold and draughty, there was no central heating in those days. The stairs were not carpeted and there was just a strip of rush matting running round the upstairs corridor, which had mullioned windows, overlooking the courtyard. Spaced out along the corridor, were wooden chests and antique wooden commodes, which were of course not used. I don't suppose the old men would have come out of their rooms at night, but like my grandfather kept a 'Jerry' under the bed. As for taking a bath in the winter, you would have had to be very tough! Now of course, each man has his own bathroom.

My grandfather's room was at the end of the corridor on the right, it had a heavy oak door with a huge key. On entering there was a heavy curtain to the right, which jutted out from the wall by about 2ft. Behind it was his single brass knobbed bed, running down by the wall. The curtain would have kept his head out of a draught. At the bottom of the bed, he had a seaman's camphor wood chest and a folding screen with paintings of the ships he had sailed around the world in when he was in the Merchant Navy as a young man There was also a lovely button backed leather armchair, next to which was his wardrobe and a door leading to his kitchen.

On the left of the entrance was a wooden screen jutting out about 3 ft. into the room. Behind it was his fireplace, above which hung a painting of himself as a young man. Next to the fire, he had a high backed wooden Windsor armchair, and a table on which he kept his wireless set.

Above the table on the wall, there was a large picture called

Grandfather's oil painting of himself when a young man.

'Belshazzar's Feast'. I didn't know who he was, but knew it was biblical it used to fascinate me, As the characters in it, all looked very frightened. I have since discovered the original painting was by Rembrandt, and is hanging in the National Gallery, in London. Belshazzar, was a Babylonian king, and had just leapt to his feet, sending guests and golden goblets flying. His eyes are bulging with terror as he stares at the glowing writing in the air, which spells the end of his life

103

Balshazzer's Feast by Rembrandt.

and kingdom. Opposite the front door was a small mullioned window overlooking the garden, with the Power station beyond it. To the left of the window, he had a tall bow fronted chest of drawers, on which stood a small beautiful Chinese cabinet, decorated with golden designs. When you opened the cabinet doors, there were lots of little drawers. We used to love to stand on a chair and look inside all the drawers in which there was a locket containing a faded lady's photograph, a lock of hair, other faded photo's, jewellery, a gold nugget, a large multi coloured Beetle shell and several other trinkets He had brought the cabinet back from his travels in China.

On the other side of the window he had a mahogany 'Chiffonier', which I am pleased to say I still have. Above it hung a glass case about 3 ft. long and about 18ins. wide which contained the ornate tail of a lyre bird, which he brought back from his travels in Australia. It was his pride and joy, when he came to live with us, he brought it with him, and hung it in his room, mother hated it, she called it his 'Blooming Feather', when he died she couldn't get rid of it quickly enough. The room was full of all his 'curios' which we loved to examine.

We also had some relations who lived at the bottom end of King William Walk, near the Old Ship Hotel. We used to sit upstairs overlooking the river. Sadly, the hotel and their house with about half a dozen others, were bombed during the war, fortunately they were not killed. The site is now occupied by the 'Cutty Sark' and 'Gypsy Moth'.

We also had some other relatives, who ran a gents out-fitters in Church Street. They had a flat above with a large drawing room, in which there was a grand piano. On Saturday or Sunday evenings, we would visit them for a musical evening. There were two sisters, one had a beautiful singing voice and she would be accompanied by her sister Alice, on the piano.

Both my older sisters had music lessons from a professor of music, who lived in Coleraine Road. Eve was taught the piano and Carole the violin. We all hated listening to them when they practised, mother would shut them up in the front room. However, Carole did quite well with the violin, and one year played with a children's orchestra at Crystal Palace. Neither of them continued with it after they left school. Mum and Dad did not think it was worth spending any money on the rest of the family for music lessons, although I did go to a little woman in the next road for lessons, which was a lot cheaper.

Crystal Palace was a place we knew quite well, as we often used to go there, it was a great place for a day out, as there were all sorts of attractions, both inside and out. They used to hold speedway races which were called 'Dirt track racing', some of the riders had nasty accidents. The men wore black leather, but no crash helmets. The smell of oil and petrol was over powering. There were also swings and roundabouts. We were very sorry when it burnt down in about 1936, it lit up the sky for miles around, we could see it quite clearly from Greenwich.

We had a gas light opposite the house, and on winter

evenings when it was dusk, we liked to sit at the front window to watch the 'lamp lighter' come round with his long pole. Also the muffin man with his tray on his head ringing a bell, we would rush out to buy some and then toast them in front of the fire. Also a 'cat's meat' man would come around with bits of meat on a skewer, it was probably horse flesh.

Quite often sitting outside the school gates there would be a man with gold fish, which you could obtain for some old rags or wool. Sometimes there would be a barrel organ at the bottom of Halstow Road.

Funerals were a magnificent affair, with an elaborate hearse, pulled by jet black horses with plumes, preceded by mutes who wore mourning suits and top hats with black silk hanging down at the back. The horses pulling the mourners carriages, were also black. My grandfather used to tell me the interior of the carriages, were always damp, and the leather upholstery smelt musty. I do not remember any coloured flowers, only wreaths made from white lilys which I still associate with death. All the neighbours pulled down their blinds or closed their curtains, on the morning of a funeral, the cortege would go very slowly, and people would stop and men raised their hats as a mark of respect. The mourners would wear black arm bands or black diamond patches sewn on to their sleeves, for months after.

On Sunday mornings, there was usually a barrow on Woolwich Road, selling shrimps, cockles, winkles and whelks, which we sometimes bought for our Sunday tea. On Sunday afternoons the 'hokey-pokey' man would come round selling El Dorado ice cream, which was delicious.

The only collections on the streets for charities, were on Poppy Day, 11th. November, when everything stopped at 11 am. for two minutes, no matter which day it fell on. The only other collection that I remember, was on Queen Alexandra Rose days, which I think was for hospitals.

Many families kept a collecting box in the house, for hospitals or the Red Cross, which we would take round to houses every so often. Also at Sunday School we were often given scent cards, which were impregnated with perfume, for ladies to put in their handbags. We would knock on peoples doors, and sell the cards for a few pence. The money we collected would go to missionary societies and other charities. If a maid answered the door, she would put it on a silver tray and take it to her mistress, and return with a few pence on the tray.

Most of the houses going up to the heath, were occupied by school-teachers, shop keepers, office managers, foremen and other skilled tradesmen, including quite a few lightermen etc. In the bigger houses on the heath, there were doctors, lawyers, accountants, City business men and stock-brokers, as well as quite a few retired naval and army officers.

Most people belonged to the H.S.A. which stood for Hospital Savings Association. If you went into hospital, which in our case was always Seaman's Hospital, there was an almoner, who would work out how much you should pay, according to your subscriptions and income. In the infirmary or Greenwich and Deptford Hospital, as it was called, in Vanbrugh Hill, I don't think there was any charge.

At the bottom of Kemsing Road, in Woolwich Road, there was a Baptist chapel, with a church hall attached to it, where we went to Sunday school. All our social life took place in there, especially in the winter. We belonged to all sorts of associations, Cubs, Brownies, Band of Hope etc. From there we went on Sunday School outings, in open topped charabancs.

Opposite was the East Greenwich Library, which had a very good children's section where we spent a lot of time. There were always plenty of books around at home, as we had grand-mothers bookcase, which was full of all the classics in French and English, many of them were first editions, which of course we did not appreciate. I remember there was one by Charlotte Bronte when she wrote under the name of Currer Bell and Dickens 'Sketches by Boz', I loved the pictures in that one, also a bound volume of 'The London Illustrated News' for 1875, there were some beautiful illustrations in that including a large one of Dr.Livingstone meeting Stanley in Africa. There were also Victorian 'Ladies Journals' with fashion plates.

We didn't often go to the cinema, as there were none near us. The Granada at the bottom of Vanbrugh Hill, hadn't been built then. There used to be a big house there with a big garden at the back, where they often held garden parties. Occasionally we went to the old Hippodrome also called Barnard's at the bottom of Crooms Hill.

We were one of the first houses in the road to have a wireless set in about 1930. I was about five or six at the time, it stood on a table in the corner of the room. I remember coming down one night for a glass of water, and finding the room full of neighbours listening to the wireless. In the evenings there was usually music, mother loved to listen to the old music hall stars singing all the old songs.

Dad used to attend St. George's Church in Kirkside Road, and I was a choir boy at St. John's Church near the Standard.

We loved going to see our grandfather, afterwards we usually walked along Crane Street, and then along the path in front of the Naval College. In the summer there were lots of families on the foreshore, and children paddling in in the river, sometimes we would go through the foot tunnel to the Isles of Dogs, but didn't stay long as there was nothing there. We then came back through the King William entrance to the park, and spent a bit of time on the round-abouts, before returning home via the gate at the top of Maze Hill.

We had a holiday every year, the first one was at Great Yarmouth, but I was too young to remember it. The first one I remember was at Cliftonville, near Margate. It was a farm owned by a friend of the family. At that time it was all fields, now it has been built over. It was where I first learnt to love the countryside and horses, as they had some big shire horses, which I liked to be lifted up on, and I enjoyed riding in the farm carts. We used to walk through the corn fields to the top of the cliffs, and then climb down to the sandy beach.

We also had some relations, an aunt and her two children,

who lived in Hunton Bridge, a little village about two or three miles north of Watford. They lived in Mill Cottage next to a mill. It had a long front garden, where my aunt grew all her own vegetables. At the rear was a small garden, under which ran a stream to the mill. We used to like to climb down to the stream to paddle. There was a low wall separating it from a meadow, which went down to the grand Union Canal, and was in full use in those days, with colourful canal barges, which we called monkey boats. They chugged along making a noise, and sometimes pulled by a horse.

The cottage was lit by oil lamps and candles, with a kitchen range and a copper. There was no running water, we had to go to the top of the front garden, where there was a tap fixed to the wall, it must have been terrible in the winter when the pipes were frozen over. There was an outside lavatory with a cesspit, in which, my cousin told me were rats. We thought it was wonderful, playing in the meadow and watching the barges going by. In the village there was a Blacksmith, I loved to watch the horses being shod.

The squire lived in a big house, about half a mile from the

Mill Cottage, Hunton Bridge right, modernised.

109

village, and wasn't liked much. All around his estate were signs saying 'Trespasses will be prosecuted'. I don't know how we crowded into the cottage, although dad didn't come as it wasn't our main holiday.

It all came to an abrupt end, when my brother and me, were trying to sail a little toy boat on the canal, when a barge went by, causing ripples, my brother found a stick, and told me to hold on to his legs, so that he could reach it. The next thing I can remember was being resuscitated in the village hall. Fortunately, a little girl, saw us both go in, and told the squire's butler who was crossing the bridge. He took off his coat and managed to pull me out, but couldn't find John, who was caught up in the undergrowth, eventually he was successful. We were very lucky, but it gave mother a terrible fright, she would never go there again, also she was not a lover of the country and found the living conditions rather hard.

In about 1931, dad rented a bungalow from a dentist at Pitsea in Essex. It was quite a large bungalow, and stood in the middle of a field, it had a large garden of about an acre. There was also a pony and governess cart, in which dad would drive us around the country lanes. We liked it so much we went again the following year. I believe it has all been built over now, and is called Basildon.

Another year, they rented a bungalow on the Sussex Downs, above Rottingdean. In the mornings we would play on the Downs, and in the afternoon, we would walk over them to the lovely old village of Rottingdean, which was quite unspoilt by tourists then. We also enjoyed that holiday, and went back the following year. After spending the afternoon on the beach, we would wend our weary way back to the bungalow. It must have been hard work for mother, as we were right out in the country, but she didn't seem to mind as long as we had a good holiday, and it was better than bed and breakfast in a boarding house.

I think the following year we had a holiday in Southsea. It was nice walking around the old town of Portsmouth, and going to the dockyard to visit Nelson's ship the 'Victory'. We also went on the ferry to the Isle of Wight.

The last family holiday we had was in 1938. Mum and dad rented a caravan at Dymchurch, it was just a small village with no amusement parks, and no sea wall, you just walked down the slipway, on to the lovely sandy beach. I remember watching a concert party performing there. We also went on the minia- ture railway to Dungeness, the power station hadn't been built then and we had some nice picnics there.

The following year 1939, mother and father took my younger sister Iris, to Scotland, we were all too old to go with them by then.

Dad's best friend Steve Fletcher, had a big open topped car with a canvas hood in the 1930's. He often took us out in in it for a picnic, usually in Kent on a Sunday. Cars didn't have boots in those days, so there was plenty of room in the back, we would all pile in, some of us sitting on the floor it was a great day out.

Every year, there used to be a regatta held on the river, in front of the Naval College, which we usually went to see, as dad sometimes took part in it, there were sailing barges and deep sea divers and a greasy pole lashed between two boats on which two men would try to knock the other one off with a bag of something.

In the 1933, the whole family took part in the Greenwich Pageant. It was a most spectacular event, and was held in the Naval College.

A huge grandstand was erected between the two buildings close to the river, and the raised area between the chapel and the painted hall, was the stage. There used to be tennis courts there before the war.

It was produced by Sir. Arthur Bryant, who was a film direc- tor and a famous historian. He was a dashing young man, and rushed around giving orders through a megaphone.

Dad played the part of one of Nelson's vice-admirals, he wore an 18th. century Naval officer's uniform made from dyed blue sack cloth, with gold braid sewn on it, and wore a cocked hat and carried a wooden ceremonial sword. Fortunately it

Greenwich Pageant, 1933.

wasn't a speaking part, in fact I don't think anybody spoke. We children and our friends were extras, we had to wear 1914 clothes, and rush on cheering and waving the troops off, when the First World War was declared. Whilst waiting to play our parts, the cast all gathered in a courtyard to the left of the stage, there were hundreds of us, all wearing different historical costumes. Some of those worn by the ladies, were beautiful, especially the Tudor ones, they were all local women, and I believe made their own. There were carriages and coaches, all made by local carpenters, everybody entered into the spirit of it.

It was on for about a week, and fortunately as far as I can remember, did not rain. It attracted visitors from far and wide, including the royal family.

At about that time, a small German Liner called the 'Monte Pascal', used to make trips from Hamburg to Greenwich with tourists. One day my eldest sister Eve, was out with her friends, when they met some young German men, one of them, whose name was Kurt, and he became friendly with Eve, and she brought him home, he was a student. The following year his parents invited her to stay with them in Berlin for a holiday. The next year which was 1939 mother invited him to stay with us for a holiday, it was to be the last two weeks in August, by then he had

Kurt Berner.

been called up in the army. He was a very good looking young man, with blond hair and blue eyes, and had a lot of charm. Unfortunately he had become indoctrinated with the Nazi philosophy, which was rather embarrassing, as we knew war was imminent, but hoped it wouldn't happen.

He once took me to the German Embassy which was in Carlton House Terrace I was very suspicious about his reasons for going there. We went to a little side door, where someone opened a little grill, and let him in, it was all rather sinister.

Mother and father with Kurt and his wife in front of the Berlin Wall.

Mother and father with me in Berlin.

At the end of August, Germany invaded Poland, and he had to return to his regiment. We saw him off from Liverpool Street Station, in a Pullman train en route to Harwich. A few days later England declared war on Germany and we did not expect to hear from him again.

At the end of the war I was with the British Army in Germany, stationed in Hanover. Every city including Berlin was flattened, and the population were starving, children were rummaging through our dustbins looking for food, and women were selling themselves for a few cigarettes, which they could barter for food.

About that time, mother had a letter from Kurt, he was living in Berlin. He had been badly wounded on the Russian Front and was now married and was anxious to know how we all were, and so we kept in touch.

Berlin had been divided into four zones, the Russians in the east, and Britain, France and America in the west. Russia did not like that, as they wanted to occupy the whole city, so they created an embargo, by closing off all the roads from the west, which we overcame by flying everything in by plane. This made the plight of the Berliners even worse, and we were asked to send them food parcels, and so mother sent parcels to Kurt and his family.

My regiment stayed in Germany for about a year, the country was in a terrible state and I never thought they would recover in my lifetime, but they all worked very hard, and within a few years they did. Kurt eventually got a job as a customs officer. By then he had two children, and was living on the outskirts of West Berlin, by the lakes.

In the 1960's, he invited my parents and myself to stay with them in Berlin, where they made us most welcome. We even crossed into East Berlin, going through the infamous 'Check Point Charlie', which was a bit scarey. We didn't enjoy it there at all, everything was so drab, and the people looked so miserable and sullen and we wandered around for hours, looking for somewhere to eat, Kurt did not come with us, he was afraid they might keep him there. When we crossed back into the West, the difference was amazing many new buildings had been built, there were lots of restaurants with tables on the pavement. The people were well dressed and the women were wearing colourful clothes and looked happy. After that they made regular visits to England, and we kept in touch until Kurt died in the 1980's.

In 1931, at the age of seven I was sent to Lombard Wall School, which was on the Woolwich Road in Charlton where I joined my brother John who was two years older than me. By then I had made quite a few friends in the neighbourhood, two brothers in particular who lived in Westerdale Road I used to call for them on the way to school, and we used to cross over Westcombe Hill, and climb over the little railway line that took goods to the river.

By then we all had roller skates and bikes, on which we often cycled to Chislehurst. We used to go via Kidbrooke, along the A20, which wasn't so busy then, to the 'Dutch house', and then along Mottingham Lane. Sometimes we would go as far as Sevenoaks.

In 1933, The Royal Hospital School moved from Greenwich to Holbrook, and my brother became one of the first pupils to go there. Mother was upset but she realised he would be receiving a better education and there were no fees to be paid as dad had served in the Royal Navy. Now it is a fee-paying school and is co-educational, and open to children without any naval connections, but if they do, then the fees are reduced.

Holbrook is about eight miles from Ipswich, on the river Stour. The reason the school moved there from Greenwich, was due to the fact that a very rich ship owner was so grateful to the Royal Navy for protecting his ships, crossing the Atlantic during the First World war, he decided to offer his Holbrook estate to the Admiralty. They handed it over to the Greenwich Hospital Trust. Mr. Gifford Sherman Reade, the benefactor, agreed with the suggestion that Greenwich Hospital School which had outgrown its quarters on the banks of the Thames,

Entrance to the Royal Hospital School, Greenwich c1910.

Entrance to the School now. Holbrook, Suffolk.

The main building of the School.

View from the river Stour.

Queen Mary's visit, being escorted by the Superintendent of School, Capt. Bruce-Gardyne, RN.

Myself, aged 14, in 1938.

should move to Holbrook.

Mr. Reade who had no heirs had decided to emigrate to New Zealand. By 1924, the scheme for the new school had been drawn up, and in 1928 the then Duke of York, later George VI, laid the foundation stone of the new school. He then sent the following message to Mr.Reade in New Zealand: "With the approval of His Majesty I have this day laid the foundation stone of the new Royal Navy Hospital School at Holbrook. Your gift of this fine open site is indeed a fitting symbol of your admiration for the work of the Royal Navy. It is my earnest hope that every success will attend your endeavour to increase, for the years to come, those benefits which were first inaugurated by Royal Charter at Greenwich two centuries ago."

Mr. Reade, who was persuaded, after seeing the plans, to change his will, leaving the whole of his fortune to Greenwich Hospital.

Sadly, Mr. Reade died in 1929, in his 85th. year, and therefore did not live long enough to his project completed which was opened in 1933. The old school buildings at Greenwich, then became the National Maritime Museum.

The new school is a magnificent collection of buildings, standing on high ground overlooking the river Stour. It has a beautiful chapel, which can seat one thousand, and one of the finest organs in the country, a large indoor swimming pool and gymnasium. There are eleven separate houses which each accommodate sixty pupils, and a flat for the housemaster and matron.

In the main building there is an assembly hall, dining hall, library and other offices as well as class rooms. There is also a purpose built village to house the other staff and their families. The whole complex stands in about fifty acres and has playing fields going down to the river, where we used to sail. I became a pupil at the school in 1936.

In our day the academic standard was pretty high, now it is very high, with most pupils going on to universities. Before the war, the discipline was very strict, it was seeped in naval tradition. Brittania ruled the waves and the Empire was intact, which we thought was going to last for ever. We had a lot to be proud of. I remember learning one of Tennyson's poems, which went:

"Not once or twice in our rough Island story,
the path of duty, was the way to glory."

We also did a lot of Kipling and Shakespeare. The school also had a very strong Christian ethos, and most boys were confirmed. In my day the school chaplain was Geoffrey Tiarks, he was a wonderful man, and came from a rich banking family. He was over six feet tall and was an Oxford Blue, he had won caps for rowing and other sporting activities, he went on to become the Bishop of Maidstone.

Of course we had no television and the wireless was only turned on for special occasions. We were sometimes shown a film in the assembly hall. We used to entertain ourselves with our various hobbies, and reading boys magazines, and in the summer play cricket. About once a month. mother came to see us, bringing a parcel including a home made cake. She would leave dad to cook the Sunday lunch for the others. It was quite a journey for her, which she did in all weathers. She would have to get a bus through Blackwall tunnel, and then a tram along Commercial Road to Aldgate, from there she would walk to Liverpool Station, and then a train to Ipswich. From Ipswich she would have to wait for a country bus to Holbrook, a journey which would take her about three or four hours. She would only be able to spend about two hours with us, before repeating the journey home. She was one of the most loving and caring of mothers'.

One year, old Queen Mary came to visit the school, and suggested it would be nice to plant some trees in the grounds. There was a wide road separating the parade ground from the playing fields so it was decided to turn it into a tree lined avenue and name it after her. She then sent all her relatives and friends to plant an oak tree. I remember our housemaster said, if you come back in fifty years time, as old men, they will be huge oak trees. Unfortunately I did not return to the school after fifty years, when I did eventually go back, the 1987 hurricane had blown most of them down, and so I did not see them in all their glory. I understand the school still have the cheque for 25/-s, that Queen Mary sent for her tree.

We had several other Royal visitors including the old Prince of Wales who flew to the school in his own plane, which he landed on the playing fields.

In 1938, at the time of the Munich crises, we filled sand bags, which we put around the infirmary. In 1939, I left school just before the outbreak of the war.

We had some marvellous Christmas's when we were children. In November mother would start to make her puddings which we would stir whilst having a wish. She would then make the cake and we would start making our paperchains. We used to buy strips of coloured paper, and mother would make us a bowl of flour and water to use as paste. A few days before Christmas, dad would bring home a huge turkey and we would all gather around the kitchen table to watch mother pluck it, cut off the head and neck, and then eviscerate it, which was a horrible job. On Christmas day there would be a roaring fire in the sitting room, we usually had a house full with relatives. After a huge Christmas dinner, we would play with our toys. At about 5pm. we had tea, the table would be laden down with cold meats, jellies, blancmanges and Xmas cake. Quite often there would be a ghost story told on the wireless. In the evening we played games and grand-dad sang lovely old Victorian ballads like; 'The Old Armchair' and 'Gathering up the shells from the seashore', as well as many others.

CHAPTER EIGHT

THE WAR YEARS 1939 – 1947

After I left school, mother took me for an interview for a job as office boy, in a firm of solicitors, that she had seen advertised in the 'Kentish Mercury'. There were quite a few other boys applying for the vacancy, but I got the job. It was a very old established firm of Greenwich solicitors, called Messrs Batchelor, Purkiss and Fry, and was above Westminster Bank opposite St. Alphege Church. It was very Dickensian, I had to sit at a high desk, with slanting sides, and brass rails above for putting ledgers, and I sat on a high stool.

There were open fires in all the rooms and I shared the enquiry office with the two shorthand typists. In the corner there was a mouth piece on the wall with a sort of cork in it with a whistle. When the boss Mr. Purkiss wanted anything, he blew down the tube in his office which was on the floor above, and I took out the cork from the mouthpiece in our office, to listen to his request. As he was a very impatient man, if you didn't get to the contraption quickly enough, he would blow again as you put your ear to it, and you would get an earful of spittle.

There was another office in London, in the Strand opposite the Law Courts, where Mr. Batchelor the senior partner worked, but he came to the Greenwich office about once a week. I often had to go up there to collect or deliver something.

I also had to go to Mr. Batchelor's House after work to take papers for him to sign, and collect them the following morning. He lived in a big house in Shooters Hill Road, where he kept a cook and a couple of maids.

They were Clerks to the Justices and Licensing Bench. Also commissioners for all the local charities. Whilst there I learnt a lot about Greenwich. I often had to accompany one of the partners to the Magistrates Court at Catford, especially if somebody was applying for a licence to sell alcohol there were usually a few cranks there, who would try to oppose it, quite often they would make such a fuss, they had to be removed from Court.

I also had to take papers to the houses of the local J.P.'s, who lived in Greenwich and Blackheath, so it was quite an interesting job. Some were working class and others more middle class, but I met some most interesting local characters. I remember one elderly gentleman who lived at the top of Vanbrugh Hill with his two unmarried daughters. He had a long beard, and always wore a smoking hat with a tassel, and he used to sit in a big armchair by the fire with his feet on a footstool, his daughters used to fuss over him all the time. I was always invited in, and used to sit and talk to him.

Another place I used to go to, was a vicarage or rectory, halfway up Blackheath Hill, it was a large detached house approached by a long drive. The vicar lived with his sister, and seemed to be a very odd couple to me. Both were tall and thin, the sister was what one would call a 'Blue Stocking' in those days, but they always invited me in. It was the coldest house I have ever been into, I was shown into a large drawing room, sparsely furnished, with very tall windows overlooking the whole of London I think the house has since been pulled down and replaced by flats.

It reminds me of when we were children. A local J.P. or other such dignitary, who lived in Coleraine Road, was very ill, and straw and sand was put on the road to deaden the sound of traffic. It was common practice in Victorian times, because of the noise of horses trotting past when we passed the house we were told to walk quietly, I can't imagine that happening these days.

The chief clerk kept telling me I should study for the law and become Articled, he gave me books to read, but I decided it was not for me.

Whilst I was there, war was declared. At first everything carried on as normal, right up to June 1940, this period was known as the 'Phoney War'. Although the Germans were fighting in Poland. Our forces the B.E.F. were in France and believed to be quite safe behind the 'Maginot Line'.

Suddenly the Germans turned their attention to the West. In a few days they swept through Holland, Belgium and Scandinavia and into France. The French and our troops put up a brave fight, but were out numbered, and pinned down at Dunkirk.

After that the war changed dramatically in England. At the office, the two male clerks were called up, and one of the typists joined the A.T.S. We prepared ourselves for the worst, but mercifully the Germans did not invade us. In September, the 'Battle of Britain' started, followed by the Blitz.

I can remember the first Air Raid vividly, it was a sunny September afternoon, we were sitting in the garden, when the sirens started to wail. We dived into our Anderson Air Raid Shelter, and all Hell was let loose. After about two hours, the 'All Clear' sounded, when we climbed out of the shelter, the sky was red, but no bombs had fallen near us, we then went to the top of Halstow Road, and saw that the whole of the Thames was on fire, from Tower Bridge to Woolwich. Hitler had decided to bomb the docks and warehouses along the river. Hundreds of people were killed. The next morning, many families from the East End, poured through Blackwall Tunnel. with their possessions in carts and prams, others came by other forms of transport.

In 1939. when war seemed imminent, every household with a garden was offered an 'Anderson Air Raid Shelter', It was named after the then Home Secretary, Sir. John Anderson. It consisted of sections of corrugated iron and was assembled in the garden. A three foot deep trench was dug, about six feet long four feet wide. We had ours placed immediately in front of dad's garden and tool shed at the bottom of the garden, earth was piled on the tunnel shaped roof, in which we planted grass seed.

When war was declared, dad cut an aperture in the side of the shed, through which we could crawl into the shelter. The shed backed on to a high wall, he then reinforced the roof. This proved to be a good idea as it meant we could use the shed to make tea and sandwiches, we had a primus stove in there and an oil lamp, also it kept us warm, as we didn't have to go straight out into the cold, and could sit in there if there was a lull in the bombing. He also made two bunks to go into the shelter so that-four of us could lie down. By the time the Blitz had started, he had joined the army, Eve was nursing and Iris had been evacuated which just left four of us, Mother Carole, John and myself.

One night an unexploded bomb dropped in the cemetery at the back of the house. The next morning we were told we had to evacuate our houses, and were directed to the 'Cecil Rooms' at the top of Marlton Street, it had been used for functions before the war. There were quite a few bombed out people there and we were given cups of tea etc. by W.V.S. ladies and other helpers. Carole, John and myself all had to go to work, so we left mother with Iris, who had returned from where she had been evacuated as she was very unhappy there.

When we arrived home from work, we thought they would have defused the bomb, it hadn't been done, and the road was sealed off. Next to the 'Cecil Rooms', a large public brick built air raid shelter had been built on some waste ground, so we decided to spend the night there. It had several entrances with passages in which the residents of the surrounding streets, stayed each night, some were sleeping on bunks and others on the floor. We sat on a form which wasn't very comfortable, with noisy children running around, also it was a pretty rough area, when the pubs closed, there was a lot of rowdy singing, also it was very stuffy. After a couple of hours, we couldn't stand it any longer, and left, the usual nightly air raid was in full swing, with bombs whistling down as well as shrapnel from our anti-aircraft guns. We went across the road to Enticknaps a large building and sheltered in a lobby there. The next day we were told, part . of the shelter had been bombed and several people were killed.

Later in the day, the parents of a friend of Iris, invited us to stay with them in Combedale Road. After one night, John and me decided to sneak past the barrier and slept in our own shelter. A couple of days later the bomb was safely defused and we were able to return home.

On another evening, the Germans dropped a lot of incendiary bombs, some landed in the garden, but one lodged in the guttering above the bathroom window and was blazing away, John rushed up to the back bedroom window. which was at right angles to the bathroom. He leant out of the bedroom window and grabbed hold of the bomb and threw it into the garden where it could do no damage, his action saved a very serious fire.

At about this time grandad came to live with us, he was in his eighties. One evening the German bombers came over later than usual, and we were all in bed, we got grandad up, but he insisted in getting properly dressed, the trouble was he had so many heavy clothes which took him a long time to put on, we then had the job of getting him downstairs and into the shelter. After that he flatly refused to go into the dug out as he used to call it. whenever we were all sitting in the shelter during an air raid, we used to worry about him upstairs in his bed, but it didn't bother him in the slightest, he had nerves of steel.

After the Christmas of 1940, the raids got less frequent, but were a lot worse, as they were dropping land mines, which did far more damage and killed a lot of people. One night after the siren had sounded we didn't bother to go into the shelter, and where sitting in the living room, when a very large bomb came down, it was like an express train going through a tunnel, we thought it was meant for us, and we all dived under the table. doors were blown off their hinges and windows came crashing in, the room was full of smoke. We rushed to the front door as we knew it had landed pretty close. Just up the road from us about six three storied houses, were just a heap of rubble. We knew many of the occupants, and knew they would have sheltered in their basements. John and me rushed up to see what we could do as did several other neighbours, but it was an impossible task trying to dig them out with our bare hands. Firemen and A.R.P. wardens all joined in, and in spite of working all night, I don't think we got anyone out alive.

Later on we had the 'Doodle Bugs' to contend with, they were terrifying, one could hear the drone of it's engine and when it stopped you knew it was going to come down, but you didn't know where, but hoped and prayed it wasn't going to land where you were, because they did tremendous damage, and usually killed a lot of people.

In spite of all the air raids and shortages of everything, it was amazing how cheerful people were, especially Londoners who could always crack a joke about things, I never heard anybody say that we should give in. There is no doubt that Churchill kept our spirits up with his famous speeches, which we looked forward to listening to. There was absolutely no doubt in his mind that we would win through, I think that was what kept us going.

The Blitz had a devastating effect on the office. First of all Mr. Purkiss who lived in Kidbrooke Park Road, was killed with all his family, by a direct hit on his house. The senior clerk had a direct hit on his house at Chislehurst and he was badly injured and blinded, he died a few months later. This was followed by the Chief Clerk, who lived at Ladywell, having his house badly damaged, and he moved with his two daughters to a hotel at Caterham, which caught fire and he was killed.

Finally the office was bombed one night, and we moved to a new premises in Crooms Hill, by then I wanted a change and joined the Civil Service, as an army auditor, with War Office. They had requisitioned an office block in Finsbury Circus, in the City.

Many times after spending a sleep-less night in the air raid shelter, I struggled to work the best way I could. I would then have to pick my way through the rubble in the City, which was becoming devastated.

I stayed in that job until I was called up in 1942 at the age of eighteen.

As far as the family were concerned, Eve my eldest sister was the first to join up. She had joined the Red Cross about a year before the war started. The local organiser lived in Vanbrugh Terrace, where Eve did her training.

On the day war was declared, September 3rd.1939, it was a Sunday, and we were filling sandbags outside Halstow Road School, for an 'Air Raid Wardens Post'. Mother and father were in Scotland with Iris our younger sister, and Eve was looking after the family.

Soon after Mr. Chamberlain made his announcement, the siren sounded, so everybody rushed to their shelters. In our case Eve took charge, and put her Red Cross-training into operation. She made us put on mackintoshes, gloves and our gas masks, in case the Germans used gas. We all sat in the shelter, expecting the sky to be black with planes, but nothing happened. It was a false alarm, after that we became quite accustomed to the air raids, and took them in our stride, but they could be pretty terrifying at times. Later, Eve reported to the Royal Herbert Hospital, at the top of Shooters Hill Road. It was designed by Florence Nightingale, and built by her friend Lord Herbert, as a Military Hospital.

Eve became a V.A.D. which stood for Voluntary Aid Detachment. This organisation was founded during the 1st. World War. for young middle and upper class ladies, who wanted to help nurse the sick and wounded. They were billeted in some houses next to the police station on the opposite corner. Eve shared a room there with Anne Bowes-Lyon, who was a cousin of the Queen. After Dunkirk, they were kept very busy.

Soon after our parents returned from Scotland, dad volunteered to join the Navy again, even though he was in a reserved occupation. But the Navy would not accept him because of his age, he was forty six. Undaunted, he went to an Army recruit-

*The grounds of the Royal Herbert Hospital. I am standing far right.
I think it was sports day, 1940.*

Eve, centre, with other V.A.D's.   *Eve with Dunkirk wounded.*

ing office, who were quite happy to accept him, and he joined the Inland Water Transport, which was part of the Royal Engineers. He was taking goods and equipment up and down rivers and canals.

On D. Day, 6th.June 1944, when we invaded Normandy. He took a heavy lifting crane across the Channel to build the famous Mulberry Harbour over there.

In 1940. my brother John, joined the Navy. he was eighteen, and served on H.M.S. Warspite, a battle ship, through-out the war. She was badly damaged on several occasions, and needed to be laid up for some urgent repairs. As there were no safe ports in England where the work could be done, as the

Germans were looking for her. The Americans came to her rescue, and allowed the repairs to be done at their Naval base at Bremerton in Seattle, on the west coast. They were there for about six months, and the Americans made a great fuss of the Ship's company, and were very hospitable. After the Warspite returned to the U.K. it was involved in more action, and finally took part in the D. Day operations, by pounding the French coast, before the landings.

Also in 1940, my sister Carole joined the W.A.A.F., I have already written about the experience she had when sleeping at Fairfax House in Beaconsfield Road. After that she was attached to Bomber Command, and stationed in Yorkshire.

As by this time the air raids were becoming less frequent. more and more children were drifting back to London. It was decided to re-open Charlton Central School and Sherrington Road. Iris, my sister became a pupil at Charlton Central School which was next to Sherrington Road School, where mother became one of the first dinner ladies, as before then, schools did not provide meals. Mother enjoyed the work and she felt she was doing her bit for the war effort.

When I was working in the City, I became friendly with a young chap, I had known at Lombard Wall School and he lived in Mycenae Road, and we travelled on the train together each morning. He told me he belonged to cycling and social club, at he top of Church Lane in Charlton, which I joined. Every Sunday, we would cycle into Kent, Surrey and Sussex and I soon made friends. On several evenings a week we used to go to the Church Hall next to 'Our Lady of Grace', a Catholic church in Charlton Road, where a dance was held.

By the time I was seventeen, I joined a couple of other friends, and we used to go to the 'Embassy Ballroom' at Welling, as they had a good band there and it was much more sophisticated. The only trouble was, that due to the war the last bus to Blackheath left at 9 pm. which was much too early

It was a long walk from Welling, over Shooters Hill. I invariably stayed at my friends house, his name was Freddie Stevens, and he lived at Charlton. He was a very good friend, and remained so, until he sadly died in 1997. We also made quite a few other friends at the Embassy, with whom we formed a rambling club. In the summer we would meet at a station, and spend the day in the country. Quite often we would get a train to Staines, where we hired two or three boats, and find a quiet spot on the river, for a picnic and swim. We had some wonderful times. Gradually the boys were called up, and my turn came in 1942, when I was eighteen.

I was sent to Colchester to do my basic training, and from there to the Royal Artillery School of Survey, at Larkhill on Salisbury Plain, where I trained to be an army surveyor. It was like being back at school again, doing maths, trigonometry and logarithms, and field work with theodolites on Salisbury Plain. I soon got used to it and made some good friends, one of whom, Peter Carrick, I am still in close contact with.

Those of us who did well, went on a more advanced course and became 'Flash Spotters'. Our job was to man an observation post, from where we could locate an enemy gun from the flash it gave when fired, and pass the information back to H.Q. When we finally passed out, we joined a Survey Regiment on the outskirts of Hull, in Yorkshire; where we trained on the moors and dales, sometimes we went up to the Northumberland moors.

In January 1944, we moved down to Sussex, and camped in

Stonehenge. L to R: Stan, Pete Boorman, Bill and myself, whilst at the 'School of Survey,' Larkhill.

Reunion, 50 years later. L to R: Pete Boorman, Peter Carrick now an author, and myself.

the grounds of a big estate called Tilgate, which belonged to Sir. Malcolm Campbell, who raced speed boats. He kept his most famous one the 'Bluebird', on one of the lakes there. It was a couple of miles from a pretty little village, called Crawley. We did a lot of hard training there, as we were preparing for the Invasion of France. Sometimes we went on a route march to a small private airport called Gatwick! One evening, the famous actress Gertrude Lawrence, came to entertain us, she was very good.

There were thousands of Americans, Canadians and British troops all around waiting for the invasion. At the beginning of June we moved down to Southampton, where we shared a camp with the Americans, and messed with them, for the first time since the war, we ate pure white bread, which was a luxury after the dirty grey stuff we had in England.

A few days after D. Day, my regiment crossed the Channel in a troop landing craft to Normandy, Whilst there, we watched the 'Doodle Bugs', cross: Channel to England, which of course did some terrible damage.

As observers, we had to be as far forward as possible, in a high position such as a Church tower or building, and sometimes in the branches of a tree, which made us a sitting target. There were four O.P's. each about one mile apart, we each had an instrument that measured angles, with powerful binoculars attached to it and a field telephone. If any of us saw a gun flash, we shouted 'Flash' ! down the phone giving the angle and estimated distance. Each of the other O.P's. would do the same, from this information, H.Q. would be able to plot the position of the enemy-gun, and pass the information on to the artillery and about five minutes later we would hear our own guns firing on the target. As the terrain was, flat, for our first O.P. the Royal Engineers built us an eighty foot high tower, using scaffold poles!

After about two months, when we had driven the Germans out of France, we swept through to Brussels, and were the first British troops to liberate the town. The inhabitants made a terrific fuss of us, and were most hospitable. Unfortunately, we couldn't stay there long, as we had to press on to Holland, where we were quite close to Arnhem, and watched the thousands of British Para-troopers, dropping down in their parachutes, most of whom were sadly killed.

After spending a bitterly cold winter in Holland, we eventually crossed the Rhine, and swept though Germany, which was in a terrible state. Every town and city was flattened, and the roads were full of German soldiers giving themselves up. Also Russians, Poles etc. who had been in slave labour camps and refugees all heading in a westerly direction.

One night we stopped to put up in a farmhouse, and were surprised to discover a little old English woman living there, she was a cockney and had been born in Woolwich, evidently she had married a German soldier after the First World War. We also passed the notorious concentration camp of Belsan, but could not stop, those who could stand up, were standing around at the gates, wearing their striped prison clothes.

We then pressed on, and eventually met up with the Russian troops, in what was to become the eastern sector of Germany, so we had to pull back. we stayed in Germany for about a year, and I was demobbed in 1947, when I was fitted out with a demob suit and given £40. most of which I spent or holiday in Jersey, where my sister was working as a receptionist in a Hotel. She had gone there for a holiday after she was demobbed from the W.A.A.F. in 1945.

Germany, 1945. Setting up checkpoints between East and West Germany, after the country was divided following the Potsdam Conference. I am in the centre.

In 1943, my other sister Eve who was a V.A.D. had married Captain Jack Essex R.A.M.C. who she had met when he was stationed as the garrison medical officer at Woolwich. He later became the M.O. at the Tower of London, which had been taken over by the army. I believe some spy's were being imprisoned there. Eve and Jack got per-

Eve's wedding to Jack at the Tower of London, 1943.
L to R: Grandpa, Mother, Carole, Dad, E ve, Jack, Best Man, myself, Iris, Jack's
brother, David and Eleanore.

mission to be married in the Chapel Royal, where Anne Boleyn and other Royal and noble personages are buried. The photographs were take on the spot where the scaffold stood. My other two sisters were bridesmaids, and dad and I were able to get leave to attend the wedding. After the war Jack, became a G.P. in Kensington.

Eve and Jack, 1945.

Dad was also demobbed as soon as the war in Europe finished, and he resumed his work with the Lighterage department at the Gas Co. My brother John, was also demobbed soon after the war, and I was the last one. During the war, the Royal Opera House, was turned into a dance hall, I used to go there when on leave. It used to be packed with British and Allied personal. The stage was removed, and a bandstand erected, on which Ivy Benson, and her all female band supplied the music.

The Gearing family at war.

CHAPTER NINE

1947-1985

After a holiday in Jersey, I soon ran out of money, and had to get a job. I couldn't decide what to do, I didn't want to go back to my old job, as I didn't want to commute London anymore, I managed to get a job at Messrs. Johnson & Phillips at Charlton, in the cost office. I thought it would do until something better turned up, but I had to wait for three years before that happened.

Whilst there, I joined the rambling club, we went out most Sundays in the summer, which was very enjoyable. I also joined their amateur dramatic club which was quite good fun.

I also had an army friend from Yorkshire, who worked in London. He was very fond of opera and classical music. Soon after the war, the Royal Opera House re-opened for opera. We saw some wonderful productions there, including 'Aida', with a cast of hundreds, it was most spectacular and we could get seats at quite a reasonable price. I used to take mother and father with me, they loved it. We also went to Saddler Wells, usually for Mozart. Also, at that time there were several operatic touring companies, who put on a lot of productions at the old Lewisham Hippodrome, which we always went to see. It is a pity it is so expensive to go to the opera now.

In 1948, our beloved grandfather died, he was just short of his ninetieth birthday, and had lived with us for the past eight

Above: *Freddie Stevens, Bob Smason and myself, 1942.*

Right: *Best man at Freddie and Rita's wedding, wearing my demob suit. Outside St. Luke's Church, Charlton, 1947.*

Best man at Bob's wedding to Jean, 1948. I am sitting far left. Bob had been a navigator with Bomber Command.

Above: *Jean, Bob and my Godson, Paul.*

Left: *Jean, Bob, Muriel and myself at a dinner. He had now joined the police force.*

A visit from Bob and Jean in Folkestone. The following year Jean died unexpectedly, and Bob died two years later.

1950. A holiday in Denmark, with some Danish friends.

years. He was a delightful man, and had white-curly hair and twinkling blue eyes, we all loved him dearly, but he was ready to go, and had no fear of death what-soever.

In 1950. my sister Carole who lived in Jersey, married the manager of the hotel where she worked, and they bought their own hotel in St. Helier. It was called the Ritz, it was quite big, and accommodated about two hundred guests. As I had been an auditor, they asked me if I would like to run the office and do the accounts and so in 1951, I took the job. I found it most interesting, and learnt a lot from my brother-in-law, who had been born in Czechoslovakia, and had trained at a hotel school in Switzerland. I also read a lot of books on food and wine, as well as learning French, as most of the staff were Continental,

Above: Carole's wedding to Charles, Greenwich Town Hall, 1950. L to R: Mother, John, Iris, Dad, Charles and Carole, Eve and myself.

Left: *Carole 1945.*

The Ritz Hotel, now demolished. The site is now occupied by a block of flats.

Right: *Charles, Carole, and me with Susie in the reception hall.*

The dining room.

The ballroom.

Myself, Carole, Iris, Eve and Jack.

Dancing with mother.

L to R: Iris, Canadian friend, myself, Carole and Eve.

Dad dancing with Carole.

With mother and Dodie.

Staff party at the end of the season. Top table L to R: Mrs. Hines, housekeeper, Leo, head waiter, Iris, myself, Dodie, head receptionist, head chef with wife and son.

Dad dancing with Iris.

Friends I made in Jersey. Danny, George, Bob and me.

Freddie and Rita with Iris and myself.

Strolling along the beach at Greve de Lecq. L to R: Myself, George, Phil and Danny.

George, myself, Pat and Donald Fullerton and Bob. George, Danny and Donald were all doctors at the general hospital in St. Helier.

1961 south of France, on the way to Rome with Danny and Alf.

Villa in Spain, with George, David and maid.

George's marriage to Pat, 1967. He is now an orthopaedic surgeon.

Iris and me in St. Helier.

and our dinner menus were always in French. I gradually learnt more about running the hotel, which stood me in good stead, as after a few years, my brother-in-law became very ill and I was able to take over as manager.

Every year our parents came over for a holiday, they loved Jersey. They also sent many of their friends from Greenwich and Blackheath to stay. Mum and dad often came at the end of the season with my sister Iris. After the hotel had closed, I would take my car over St. Malo, and we would drive across France and spend the night in Paris. From there we would go down to the south of France. On another occasion we drove all over Italy going to Rome, Naples and Venice. One year we drove through Switzerland, another time we went Austria, and stayed in Vienna for a few days. whilst we were where we went to the new Opera House, where we saw 'Tanhauser'.

The 1950's, was a wonderful time to travel on the Continent, as there were very few tourists, hotels and petrol was cheap, and English people were made very welcome, also there were no motorways, so that that one could enjoy the scenery and vil-

Ma and Pa in Dinard, France. 1954.

...and at the top of the Eifel Tower.

The Church of Moindeville Caen, Normandy. During the war, I had to man an observation post at the top of the 180ft. tower, which was badly shelled.

Ma nd Pa in a gondola, 1953.

Above: *Mother being arrested by the Venetian police.*

Right: *Dad trying his hand at being a Gondolier.*

With Iris and mother in St. Marco Square.

Crossing the Simplon Pass, Italy.

Bellagio, Lake Como, Italy. With the family of Aldo the chef at the Ritz. 1954.

Eagles nest at Berchesgarten, Bavaria, Hitler's home.

Above: *Vienna, Ma and Pa standing in front of Strauss's statue.*

Right: *St. Moritz, Switzerland. 1954.*

Above: *St. Moritz, Switzerland. 1956.*

Right: *With Philip, the head waiter at the Ritz, in the summer, and Palace Hotel, St. Moritz, winter.*

lages we passed through.

Mothers' favourite city was Venice, when we came back from Italy, her niece gave her a budgerigar, as a birthday present, which she named 'Venny'. Mother would talk to the bird for hours, and taught it all the nursery rhymes, as well as many other comical expressions, such as "Shut the door Jack", when dad came into the room, or "wash your hands, Jack" if he had been in the garden also it would fly around the room saying "Can't find me"! Venny gave mother and the rest of the family a great deal of pleasure.

Aboveand right: *Menton, south of France. 1953.*

Below: *St. Gothard Pass. Iris standing by my 'Triumph Renown'.*

In 1960, due to ill health, my brother-in-law, sold the hotel, and I decided I would like a change, and bought a restaurant in St. Helier. It had a two bedroom house attached to it, and fifteen bedrooms above in which the previous owners, had taken in visitors for bed and breakfast, but I turned them into studio flats.

At the same time, dad retired from the gas works, after forty years. As mum and dad had always loved Jersey, they said they would like to retire to the island, and so they came over to live in the house I had next to the restaurant and they wanted to help me set up my new business. Dad became the maintenance man, and converted the rooms into studio flats, and mother made cakes and puddings in her little kitchen to sell in the restaurant. They thoroughly enjoyed themselves, it made a great change for them. After a while they got their own flat nearby, where they could have their own friends and relatives

Above: *White Jag, to match Smokey.*

Left: *Cadora Restaurant. Smokey and Fluffy. 1960's.*

Below: *With Joe O'Donnell at a Mansion House dinner.*

to stay with them.

My sister, Iris was about to get married when they left, and so she and her husband stayed on at Humber Road, which had been converted into flats by then.

I used to come over to England quite frequently staying in Humber Road. The local history library, at 'Woodlands' had just opened, and I used to visit it quite a lot and developed an interest in my own family history. At about this

time my other sister Carole whose husband Charles had died soon after they sold the hotel in Jersey, where a few years later, on a visit to Blackheath. She met Joe O'Donnell who owned the 'Clarendon' and 'Westcombe Park' Hotels. He was also a builder and property developer, had recently lost his wife, who had run the hotels. After a while, Carole offered to come over

145

1967, my mother and father celebrate their golden wedding anniversary, 50 years, and their first grandchild is born, which mother had waited so long for.

Christening of Jennifer Jane Tuff, at Otford, Kent.

Above: *With Eve and dad.*

Left: *Twin boys are born to Iris and John, and Christened Anthony Henry Tuff and Simon James Gearing Tuff, with Iris, John and Jennifer.*

to help Joe run the 'Westcombe Park Hotel'. His son Michael was running the 'Clarendon'. Eventually, Joe sold the 'Westcombe Park Hotel', to the Chinese Embassy, and he came to live with Carole in Jersey, leaving Michael at the 'Clarendon', and his other son Patrick, managing the property Joe owned around Blackheath.

After running the restaurant for ten years, I decided to sell it in 1970. Dad still wanted something to do, although he was in his late 70's. My eldest sister Eve, who had lost her husband, and had no children, had bought a large house in Lee, which she was converting into flats and dad wanted to help her. Also my other sister Iris, who was now living in Otford, Kent, had started a family and now had three young children, Jennifer, and twin boys Anthony and Simon. Mother wanted to be near them, as they were her first grandchildren, and so they returned to Blackheath. They moved into a nice flat in Montpelier Row, opposite 'All Saints Church', where dad became a regular worshipper and sidesman. Also they still knew a lot of people in the area, and dad liked being near the river again, and was able to make contact with the few old workmates who were still alive.

He also joined the 'Gallipoli Association', Which had recently formed for the veterans of that ill-fated campaign. It gave him an interest, which he became very involved in. On 'Anzac', day 25th.April, each year he would attend a ceremony at the Cenotaph in Whitehall, with other veterans, and lay wreaths, along with representatives from Australia and New Zealand. Followed by a beautiful service in Westminster Abbey, after which, they had-a lunch. He made many friends there, but sadly over the years, they all died off, eventually leaving him as the sole survivor. On their behalf and in memory of those who had perished in that terrible campaign, he carried on laying a wreath until he was one hundred and two years old. Fortunately many of their sons and grandsons of men who had fought there, and other who were interested joined the association, of which I am one, the membership is increasing.

Dad was now in his eighties and Eve didn't need him anymore, but he still wanted something to do, and so he decided to make a model of his father's sailing barge, 'The Star'. It was the one he served on in the early part of his apprenticeship. He did the whole thing from memory, by himself, none of us knew

Marching down Whitehall on Gallipoli Day 25th April.

Dad laying a wreath at the Cenotaph.

how he did it, as he wasn't a carpenter, and he had never tackled any skilled crafts before.

He made a perfectly shaped wooden hull about two feet long which he painted black, he then put in the decks and hatches, also the mast all to scale. Many of the other intricate details that he added were improvised, and made to look the real thing. He bought some canvas for the sails which he cut to shape and mother sewed and he painted them brown. It took him a few years to complete, and he finished it by the time we moved to Folkestone when he was ninety.

When he was one hundred, it came to the attention of 'The Company of Watermen and Lightermen', that he was the oldest lighterman they had ever heard about, he was invited to a reception at Watermens Hall in the city of London. As I did not know what would become of the model after we had all gone, I suggested to him that he might like to present it to them, which he thought was a very good idea.

When we arrived there, we were met by the master in his full robes of office, the Queen's head 'barge master' and the other elders of the company. They were delighted to have the 'barge'. I was surprised to discover they did not have one. He also presented them with an album of photographs, and written descriptions of his life on the river, which was compiled by my sister Eve. They found this very interesting, as they did not possess any such records. Also he was the only man still alive, who had served on a Thames working sailing barge.

Whilst he was working on his 'barge', the arthritis in mother's knees was getting worse and very painful. And so he did all the shopping and cooking, something he had never done before, but he became quite a good cook. Sticking mainly to fried or grilled steak, boiled gammon, Dover soles and smoked salmon, as they had a very good butcher and fishmonger in Blackheath Village so we always ate well when we visited them!

After I sold the restaurant, I bought a lovely old 18th century granite house, called Bulford close to the beach in Jersey, by

149

Dad presenting his model sailing barge to the Master of the Company of Watermen and Lightermen, with Bob Crouch, at Watermens Hall in the City.

Standing in front of the Company's Coat of Arms.

150

a quiet sandy bay, on the south side of the island. It was big enough to accommodate Mum and Dad, who would stay with me for a few months during the summer. Also when the school holidays started, Jennifer my niece would come to join us. Her mother would put her on a plane and we would meet her. She loved it there, and I taught her to ride 'Polly', the horse I owned. A couple of weeks later, her parents used to bring the two boys, Anthony and Simon, so we had quite a house full. Fortunately I had a self-contained flat, which I used to let to visitors. We had some wonderful family holidays, and it gave Mother-and Father a great deal of pleasure.

In 1977, our parents celebrated their Diamond Wedding, sixty years. The O'Donnell family, kindly arranged a party for them at the 'Clarendon Hotel'. We got in touch with as many

Bulford House, St. Clement, Jersey. 1970.

Mother, with Jennifer and her father, John, on the beach.

Lunch in the garden. L to R: Mother, father, Iris, John Anthony, Simon and Jennifer.

Jennifer with the twins on the beach.

151

Jennifer with the two boys in the garden.

Myself with the three children, Sark.

All having a trip around Sark on a horse and wagon.

Jennifer.

Jennifer, a little older with Ma and Pa, riding Polly.

Jennifer, bigger still, with Anthony and Simon.

old friends and neighbours, they had known before the war, in most cases it was their children, who had been our playmates, in all they numbered about two hundred.

Before the celebrations took place, Mum and Dad said they would like to re-take their vows at Christ Church where they had married in 1917, The vicar of 'All Saints' on Blackheath

Above: *Myself, hunting with the Jersey Drag Hounds. There are no foxes on the island.*

Right: *Our parents Diamond Wedding Anniversary, 60 years, entering Christ Church, Greenwich, before it was altered, to re-take their vows. 1977.*

arranged with the vicar at Christ Church to conduct the service. Christ Church hadn't been altered then. All the guests were invited to come to the service, we then adjourned to 'The Clarendon Hotel', the party was a great success. Our German friend Kurt brought his son over to join in the celebrations.

By the early 1980's, after having lived in Jersey for thirty years, I decided to sell up, and return to England. Also Mum and Dad were both ninety and mother had great difficulty in walking due to arthritis. Dad was having to do everything for her. None of the family lived near them, the nearest was Iris who lived at Orpington, but she had three young children. Eve and my brother John and his wife, were all living in Folkestone.

To begin with, I managed to rent a flat in Blackheath, which wasn't very satisfactory. On a visit to Folkestone with my parents, I came across a large two bedroomed ground floor flat for sale. It had a nice garden, and direct access to the famous 'Leas', a beautiful grass promenade at the top of the cliffs. Mum and Dad fell in love with it, and so we moved there in 1985. It was part of a large Victorian house, and quite spacious, so we were not on top of each other.

Family group outside the church. L to R: myself, Eve, John, Dad, June (John's wife), Mother, Carole, Joe O'Donnell, Iris and John Tuff, with Simon, Anthony and Jennifer.

Above: *Ma and Pa cutting the cake at the reception a the Clarendon Hotel, Blackheath.*

Right: *Mother with Jennifer.*

154

Above: *John Tuff with Mateus, his father Kurt, Iris and Anthony.*

Right: *Kurt with dad.*

Aveney Court, Folkestone. 1980's.

Carole, dad, Eve, Iris, mother and John, in the garden.

It was absolutely ideal for our needs. Mother now needed a wheel chair, every morning when the weather was fine dad would take her out in it. He did not have to cross any roads to get on to the 'Leas', which is about a mile long, and has a concrete path running along the length of it. We lived at the far end, and dad took her right to the end and back again usually stopping for a coffee. He was still doing it for the next ten years when they were both one hundred! In the afternoons, after lunch, they would have a nap, and they would either sit in the garden, or he would take mother out again. Dad loved living by the sea, also

Dad taking mother down the garden path.

Sitting outside the flat.

On the leas, with Aveney Court in the background.

we were close to my brother and sister and wasn't far for Iris to come down with the children. Also I used to take them out at least once a week in the car, when we would explore the Kent country side, or go to Sussex where we had some friends.

CHAPTER TEN

FOLKESTONE 1985 – 1997

One of the advantages of me living with our parents, meant that Dad could now go to his Gallipoli functions without worrying about mother being left on her own.

Soon after moving to Folkestone a retired Brigadier, who lived in the town, got in touch with us. He was the President of the 'Old Contemptible Association', a First World War association, although he wasn't an 'Old Contemptible'. The Brigadier invited dad to become an honorary member of the organisation.

Brig. Sprake had served very bravely in the Second World War, having been awarded the M.C. and M.M. We didn't discover this until after he had died, as he was such a modest man. He was a wonderful man, and became a great friend of ours. He was also a friend of the Queen Mother. He was an architect by profession, and had been responsible for modernising Buckingham Palace after the war, and used to have lunch with the King and Queen once a week. The Queen Mother became Patron of the Association. Through the Brigadier, dad met Her Majesty on several occasions, and she always asked how the 'Old Gentleman' of Folkestone was. This culminated in a visit to Clarence House with some other veterans where we had tea with Her. I was also invited, it was a wonderful occasion, and

Above: *Dad meeting Margaret Thatcher. Brig. Sprake is standing next to her.*

Right: *Dad with Field Marshall Lord Brammall.*

Eve, Brig. Sprake and Dad.

Dad meeting Her Majesty the Queen at a garden party at Buckingham Palace, I am standing next to dad.

we felt completely relaxed with Her. Whilst there, Her Lady-in-Waiting, made a note of the dates of my parents birthdays and wedding anniversary. From then on they received a greeting on each occasion and a Christmas card. We also received a beautiful letter of condolence when each of them died.

The Brigadier also arranged for us to go to two garden parties at Buckingham Palace. He organised a visit to the House of Commons, and to have tea with Margaret Thatcher at Ten Downing Street afterwards.

He also took the veterans to the Royal Tournament and Trooping of the Colour each year. Sometimes he would hire a coach and take them out for the day in Kent. He did all this, in spite of being crippled with arthritis which was caused through being tortured by the Germans, after being captured by them behind enemy lines.

One of the veterans dad met, was also a Greenwich man, he had been born above a shop opposite East Greenwich Baths. Both were born on the same day and had both married girls named Thompson from Bermondsey.

In 1987, Mum and Dad celebrated their platinum wedding anniversary, 70 years. This time we had a reception in a Folkestone hotel, and invited many friends from Greenwich and Blackheath. In 1992, we celebrated their 75th. anniver-

Dad meeting Her majesty the Queen Mother.

Jack and May celebrating their platinum wedding, 70 years. 1987

With Michael Howard, M.P., for Folkestone.

159

sary, as the numbers were dwindling we had a party in the flat.

During all this time they both enjoyed good health, hardly ever seeing a doctor, and they never took medication. The last time they were ill, was when they were living in Blackheath, when dad had three hernias, the last one was operated on, under local anaesthetic. I think the hernias were due to the fact that he had to lift mother in and out of the bath. Also at Blackheath mother developed a melanoma on her right fore finger, and had to have it amputated at Greenwich hospital, also performed under a local anaesthetic. She took it in her stride, and soon got used to writing without it, They bred them tough in those days!

In 1993, mother celebrated her 100th.Birthday, which called for another party.

Also in 1993, we were contacted by the Imperial War Museum, to say they were putting on an exhibition called 'Forces Sweethearts', which was about wartime weddings. They advertised for couples who had been married during the war, to send them their wedding dresses if they still had them. Quite a few were able to do so. Some were interviewed by the actress Joanna Lumley, as she was writing a book about it.

During the preparations for the exhibition it was brought to the Museum's attention, that there was a couple still alive who had been married during the First World War. When I told them, mother still had her wedding dress, that was a bonus, and they asked me to send it them. They also said they would like Mum and Dad to come as guests of honour.

On the morning of the exhibition a chauffeur driven car was sent for us. When we arrived at the museum, Mum and Dad were treated like royalty, The place was packed with V.I.P.'s and celebrities who all made a terrific fuss of them. The press took lots of photo's of them with Joanna Lumley. When the exhibition ended about six weeks later, we were invited there again as they were putting on fashion show of all the costumes. They had found a nice little model to wear mother's, and it looked beautiful on her, mother was thrilled to see it worn again after

The couple with Joanna Lumley who is holding May's wedding dress.

Forces couple's 75-year marriage

A COUPLE who met in 1912 and have been married for 75 years were guests of honour at yesterday's celebrity launch of an exhibition on forces sweethearts.

Jack and May Gearing, of Folkestone, Kent, are thought to be the oldest forces sweethearts in the country.

May (99) brought along the silk wedding dress she wore in November 1917 to add to the exhibition at the Imperial War Museum in London.

The course of true love did not run smooth at first for the couple. Jack (98) broke off the relationship when he joined the Royal Navy at the start of the first world war.

"I did not want to get married in case I got killed," he said.

Undeterred, May asked his mother for his address so she could write to him.

Jack was impressed and told his mother, "Tell her not to write but to put up the banns so we can get married on my next leave."

Jack admitted, "We have had our ups and downs but I always made sure we made it up before I went to bed. That is my advice to the younger generation."

The Forces Sweethearts exhibition opens to the public today until October.

seventy five years!

By now mother and father were becoming celebrities themselves due to their longevity and the record breaking length of their marriage.

Dad was also becoming famous as one of the last survivors

Abobe: *Sitting with mother in Iris's garden.*
Left: *With model, Sophie, wearing mother's wedding dress.*

Jennifer, Carole, John Tuff, Eve and Iris on Blackheath.

of Gallipoli, and having served in the navy in the First World War and the army in the Second. The local Folkestone press took quite an interest as did the 'Kentish Mercury', who wrote some very nice articles about them.

One day I received a phone call from an author, Max Arthur who was a military and naval historian and had written sever-

162

Above: *May and Jack,*

Left: *Mother celebrates her 100th birthday, 11th November 1993.*

al books. He asked if he could come down to interview dad. Which he did and taped some of his naval experiences at Gallipoli and elsewhere, as he was writing a book about the Royal Navy during the First World War. When the book was published, it was called 'The True Glory', and dad's picture in his naval uniform is on the cover. Also Max Arthur arranged for the book to be launched after publication, at the Imperial War Museum. Once again we were invited there for the occasion, as were the press, from all the papers and they were interviewed by their reporters. Max asked dad to quote some Shakespeare to them which he did, a speech by Cardinal Wolsey, from Henry VIII. This was followed by an encore when he sang a little song they sang during the First World War about Charlie Chaplin. The Press men were amazed and there was a big writeup in the 'Times', 'Telegraph' and other papers the next day, dad was 101 years old at the time!

In 1994, mother sadly died peacefully at home after a short illness, she was in her 101st year. Dad, my brother and myself were with her. I was thankful she did not have to go into a home, apart from the war years, she had never been separated from my father.

We received many cards and letters of condolence, including the one from the Queen Mother.

Dad missed her terribly, after nearly seventy-seven years of marriage, I was glad I was able to be with him, which I think helped to keep him going for another three years. In fact I enjoyed the years they lived with me, they were no trouble, and never grumbled or complained about anything, they had been like that all their lives. If anyone sympathised with mother about her arthritis, which gave her a lot of pain, she always said there were others worse. I shall always be grateful that I was able to provide them with a home, and be there when they needed me. For various reasons, it was not possible for other members of the family, to look after them, and none of us wanted them to go into a home. I was determined not to let that happen, as they had been such wonderful parents, and had made many sacrifices for us when we were young.

In September 1994 dad celebrated his 100th Birthday, which meant more cards and letters, and another telegram from the

Dad celebrates his 100th birthday, 8th September, 1994. Back row, L to R: Myself, John, Iris, Anthony, cousin Barbara, cousin Sylvia, Michael O'Donnell. Front: Mayor of Greenwich, Dad, Eve, Carole.

Dad with cousin Barbara and Peggy Freake. Peggy used to have a florist shop on Trafalgar Road, Greenwich. Her parents, Mr. and Mrs. Flory, had a greengrocers opposite East Greenwich Library. Peggy is also a cousin of Lewis's, the coach firm in Greenwich, who were also at the party.

Dad's 101st birthday, drinking champagne before boarding the Eurostar train. 1994.

Lunch at the chateau about 20 miles from Calais.

Iris and me going to a banquet at the Painted Hall to celebrate the 300th anniversary of the founding of Greenwich Hospital.

Queen and Queen Mother. We have quite a selection now. For dad, we had a party at the Clarendon Hotel, at Blackheath, as some of our old friends would have found it too difficult to get to Folkestone. Among the many guests, was the Mayor of Greenwich and Woolwich.

On dad's 101st Birthday in 1995, my three sister's and

Jennifer marries Luke Pascal Blades Williamson in Florida on dad's birthday, 8th September.

Simon and Anthony going to a Gallipoli dinner.

myself, took him through the Channel Tunnel, which had recently opened. He was the oldest person who had ever been through it. In recognition of this, we were presented with a bottle of champagne to celebrate, and an announcement was made over the tannoy, and many people came along to congratulate him. We drove down to a chateau about twenty miles from Calais for lunch, and returned in the evening.

In November 1995, the Duke of Edinburgh unveiled a plaque in St. Pauls Cathedral. As it was the 80th anniversary of the Gallipoli Campaign and dad was asked to take part in the ceremony, by giving the exhortation:

"They shall grow not old, as we that are left grow old.
Age shall not weary them, or the years condemn,

At the going down of the sun, and in the morning,
We will remember them".

He stood up unaided and said these word, from memory, without any mistakes, in front of a packed assembly of the 'Great and the Good', at the age of 101 years with a loud clear voice that amazed all those present we were very proud of him. Afterwards the Duke of Edinburgh came over to congratulate him, and all the high ranking chiefs of staff, queued up to shake his hand.

During 1995, I had taken him by boat to Jersey to stay with my sister Carole, who had recently lost her husband Joe O'Donnell. It was a very rough crossing and. many people were ill, but dad enjoyed every minute of it. At about that time, my brother John, had lost his wife June, and Iris had lost her husband John a few years earlier. But the Gearing tribe were still battling on, as we are at the time of writing this. When mother

Dad celebrates his 102nd birthday, and Jennifer and Luke have his first great grandchild. Baptised Emily May, named after my mother who was May Emily. He is holding the baby with Luke and Jennifer in the background.

Above: *Jennifer, dad, Iris and little Emily.*

Left: *Dad nursing Emily wearing mother's wedding dress, now a Christening gown, in St. Ann's Gardens.*

was alive, she and Dad and their five children, were all drawing their 'Old Age' pensions!

In March 1996, the first great grand child was born, in New Jersey, U.S. to Jennifer Jane and her husband Luke. Jennifer was the daughter of my sister Iris. Luke came from Orpington and had worked on the London Stock Exchange. In 1990, Luke was transferred to the New York Stock Exchange. Jennifer went with him, and they were married in Florida, on the eighth of September 1992, which was dad's ninety-eighth birthday. On his one hundred and second birthday, the new baby was Christened Emily May, after her great grandmother, May Emily, in mother's dress, which had been made into a Christening gown. Dad was able to hold little Emily during the ceremony. 'The Daily Telegraph', sent a reporter and camera man who took a lovely photograph of the event, which duly appeared in their paper with a story. It was a testament of the great love and affection, Jennifer had for her grand parents.

In October 1996, I took dad to the Gallipoli lunch, which was held at the Naval Club, in Mayfair. At the commencement of the meal, dad was able to stand up and give the exhortation, as he had done for the past thirty years. He was getting very fee-

Above: *Dad with Luke's brothers, John, Luke and Guy.*

Right: *Dad spending his last Christmas in a nursing home.*

ble. When we arrived home, I was helping him up the two steps to the front door, when he slipped and I couldn't hold him. He fell heavily, cracking his pelvis. Whilst in hospital he caught a bug, and slowly went downhill. In December, we had him transferred to a nursing home in Folkestone. The family were with him on Christmas Day, when he perked up, but during January

Surrounding dad's bed, L to R: Anthony, John, Simon, Carole, Eve and Iris.

1997, he became very weak. On the night of the 27th. My two sisters, Eve and Carole, with myself, were with him all night, and he died peacefully at six o'clock on the morning of the 28th January 1997.

We gave dad a full military funeral, which was held at 'Holy Trinity Church', where he had worshipped from the time of his arrival in Folkestone until his last accident.

The Union Flag was draped over the coffin, and his medals placed on a cushion on top. The pall bearers were his two

Dad's funeral. Anthony carrying the coffin at the front, Simon's legs can be seen at the back in the centre. 10th February 1997.

Above: *Royal Marines bugler.*

Left: *British Legion with their banners.*

grandsons, Anthony and Simon Tuff. Also two men from the Royal Navy Association, who had served on a later ship called the 'Theseus', which was involved in the Korean War. About a dozen members of the British Legion attended with their flags. A Royal Marine bugler, came from his depot in Portsmouth, and played the 'Last Post', which was very moving in that large church. The church was filled with people who came from different parts of England, including the Mayor of Folkestone. The Chairman of the Gallipoli Association gave a very moving address. Followed by Max Arthur, who read from his book 'The True Glory', some of Jack's experiences whilst serving in the Royal Navy. He also read one of Jack's favourite Shakespearian quotations, from a speech by Cardinal Wolsey. Henry VIII, Act 3 Scene 2.

"farewell? A long farewell to all my greatness,
This is the state of man; today he puts forth
The tender leaves of Hope; tomorrow blossoms,
and bears his blushing honours thick upon him;
The third day comes a frost, a killing frost.
and, when he thinks, good easy man, full surely
His greatness is a ripening, nips his root and then he
falls as I do".

A great friend of Jack's, Mr, Lewis Jones, read from Ecclesiasticus.
I then read 'Crossing the Bar', from Tennyson's 'In Memoriam'. Dad loved this poem, he read to us when we were children, as his mother had read it to him when he was a boy.

Sunset and evening star,
and one clear call for me!
and may there be no moaning of the bar,
When I put out to sea.
But such a tide as moving seems asleep,
Too full for sound and foam,
When that which drew from out the boundless deep
Turns again home,
Twilight and evening bell.
and after that the dark!
and may there be no sadness of Farewell,

When I embark;
For tho' from out our bourne of time and place
The flood may bear me far,
I hope to see my pilot face to face
When I have crossed the bar.

Wreaths were laid by representatives of the various organisations Jack was involved with, around the coffin.

The Royal Navy Association.

The Royal Engineers Association.

The Gallipoli Association.

The Old Contemptibles Association.

H.M.S. Thesius Mk.3 Association.

The R.N. Benevolent Association.

and

The Company of Watermen and Lightermen of the River Thames.

Their wreath was laid by one of the Queen's Bargemen, wearing his scarlet regalia, and his 'Doggett's Badge'.

This was followed by the Bugler playing the 'Last Post', and Lt. Col. Gladstone gave the 'Exhortation'.

With our father's passing, it was the end of an era, having been born in 1894, Queen Victoria was still on the throne and he had seen her open Blackwall Tunnel. When he was a boy, most houses were lit by oil lamps and candles. Gas cookers had only recently been invented, and women cooked by a kitchen range. Motor transport was in it's infancy, and he had travelled by horse

Emily standing by the place of internment of Jack and May's ashes in Clayton churchyard, where he joined many of his ancestors.

172

View of the South Downs from Clayton Church.

tram to London and Woolwich. Aircraft had not been invented, and telephones were not in general use. There were no radios and television and computers were unheard of. Life was much more leisurely, although most working people worked very hard and there was terrible poverty.

Jennifer and Luke's home in New Jersey, U.S.A.

Jack was one of the last men to have served his apprenticeship on a working Thames sailing barge, which was very hard work, especially in bad weather, when the ropes and sails were frozen. There were no set hours, they worked according to the tides, and could be away for several days at a time.

In spite of the hard work, Jack loved his job. The River Thames was in his blood, which he had inherited from his forefathers, of whom he was very proud, but sad to know that he was the last member of the 'Gearing' family who had worked on the river in an unbroken chain of four generations, covering a period of nearly two hundred years!

Christmas 2000. Emily with
her baby brother, John Henry
Blades Williamson, the latest
addition to the family.

Visit by Jennifer to England, with Emily, Simon,
Iris, Jennifer, Anthony and Carole.

I should like to end, with part of the address, given by Capt. Christopher Fagan, the Chairman of the Gallipoli Association, at Jack's funeral;

"I came to know Jack through the Gallipoli Association, whose object is to keep alive the memory of the Campaign and all who took part in it, and lessons to be learned from it. We meet twice a year, and Jack has never missed a single event, in the thirty years he has been a member. On Gallipoli Day, 25th.April, at a ceremony at the Cenotaph organised by the Australian and New Zealanders, Jack has laid a wreath on behalf of the Association, it is remarkable that he was still doing so, on his feet at the ages of 100 and 101. At our lunches afterwards, grace in the form of the exhortation, has always been said by Jack, with a rousing 'All together now!' when it came to saying 'We will remember them'. We were often entertained by his stories and anecdotes of his experiences, and were sometimes treated to passages from Shakespeare, amazingly recited by heart. Sometimes he would be keen to get up and say his piece, slightly at the wrong time, and quietly told by Eve or Albert 'Not yet dad', and he would sit down with that delightful smile that we all grew to know and love. He was a delightful person, always cheerful, and a true gentleman. We shall miss Jack enormously".

The Christening of John Henry Blades Williamson at St. Nicholas Church, Arundel, West Sussex, on 18th February 2001. Great grandson of Jack and May Gearing.

Outside the church of St. Nicholas, Arundel, West Sussex. Parents, Luke and Jennifer with their children, Emily May and John Henry.

What seems to come through loud and clear, with Jack's actions and his writings, is that he was a man proud of his British lineage, proud of his Country and his family, a devoted Husband and perhaps above all a committed Christian with a deep-seated care and concern for others.

The best memorial that we can give him is not to forget, and so, with all my heart I say to Jack, "Thank you, and we will remember you".

FROM SUSSEX YEOMAN TO GREENWICH WATERMEN

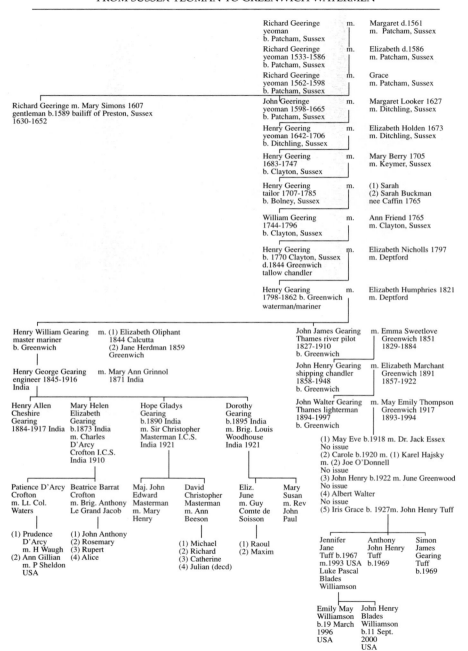

Richard Geeringe — m. — Margaret d.1561
yeoman
b. Patcham, Sussex — m. Patcham, Sussex

Richard Geeringe — m. — Elizabeth d.1586
yeoman 1533-1586 — m. Patcham, Sussex
b. Patcham, Sussex

Richard Geeringe — m. — Grace
yeoman 1562-1598 — m. Patcham, Sussex
b. Patcham, Sussex

John Geeringe — m. — Margaret Looker 1627
yeoman 1598-1665 — m. Ditchling, Sussex
b. Patcham, Sussex

Henry Geering — m. — Elizabeth Holden 1673
yeoman 1642-1706 — m. Ditchling, Sussex
b. Ditchling, Sussex

Henry Geering — m. — Mary Berry 1705
1683-1747 — m. Keymer, Sussex
b. Clayton, Sussex

Henry Geering — m. — (1) Sarah
tailor 1707-1785 — (2) Sarah Buckman
b. Bolney, Sussex — nee Caffin 1765

William Geering — m. — Ann Friend 1765
1744-1796 — m. Clayton, Sussex
b. Clayton, Sussex

Henry Geering — m. — Elizabeth Nicholls 1797
b. 1770 Clayton, Sussex — m. Deptford
d.1844 Greenwich
tallow chandler

Henry Gearing — m. — Elizabeth Humphries 1821
1798-1862 b. Greenwich — m. Deptford
waterman/mariner

Richard Geeringe m. Mary Simons 1607
gentleman b.1589 bailiff of Preston, Sussex
1630-1652

Henry William Gearing — m. (1) Elizabeth Oliphant
master mariner — 1844 Calcutta
b. Greenwich — (2) Jane Herdman 1859
— Greenwich

Henry George Gearing — m. Mary Ann Grinnol
engineer 1845-1916 — 1871 India
India

Henry Allen
Cheshire
Gearing
1884-1917 India

Mary Helen
Elizabeth
Gearing
b.1873 India
m. Charles
D'Arcy
Crofton I.C.S.
India 1910

Hope Gladys
Gearing
b.1890 India
m. Sir Christopher
Masterman I.C.S.
India 1921

Dorothy
Gearing
b.1895 India
m. Brig. Louis
Woodhouse
India 1921

Patience D'Arcy
Crofton
m. Lt. Col.
Waters

(1) Prudence
D'Arcy
m. H Waugh
(2) Ann Gillian
m. P Sheldon
USA

Beatrice Barrat
Crofton
m. Brig. Anthony
Le Grand Jacob

(1) John Anthony
(2) Rosemary
(3) Rupert
(4) Alice

Maj. John
Edward
Masterman
m. Mary
Henry

David
Christopher
Masterman
m. Ann
Beeson

(1) Michael
(2) Richard
(3) Catherine
(4) Julian (decd)

Eliz.
June
m. Guy
Comte de
Soisson

(1) Raoul
(2) Maxim

Mary
Susan
m. Rev
John
Paul

John James Gearing — m. Emma Sweetlove
Thames river pilot — Greenwich 1851
1827-1910 — 1829-1884
b. Greenwich

John Henry Gearing — m. Elizabeth Marchant
shipping chandler — Greenwich 1891
1858-1948 — 1857-1922
b. Greenwich

John Walter Gearing — m. May Emily Thompson
Thames lighterman — Greenwich 1917
1894-1997 — 1893-1994
b. Greenwich

(1) May Eve b.1918 m. Dr. Jack Essex
No issue
(2) Carole b.1920 m. (1) Karel Hajsky
m. (2) Joe O'Donnell
No issue
(3) John Henry b.1922 m. June Greenwood
No issue
(4) Albert Walter
No issue
(5) Iris Grace b. 1927 m. John Henry Tuff

Jennifer
Jane
Tuff b.1967
m.1993 USA
Luke Pascal
Blades
Williamson

Anthony
John Henry
Tuff
b.1969

Simon
James
Gearing
Tuff
b.1969

Emily May
Williamson
b.19 March
1996
USA

John Henry
Blades
Williamson
b.11 Sept.
2000
USA